SUREFIRE

SALES CLOSING TECHNIQUES

Les Dane

dreit

303 335
3304

cul 303 589 1956

Parker Publishing Company, Inc.
West Nyack, N. Y.

Library of Congress
Catalog Card Number: 78-135891

Originally published as

Big League Sales Closing Techniques

20 19 18 17 16 15 14 13

How This Book Will Do
MIRACLES for You

Webster says that to close means "to shut off; to remove from the presence of, as in closing a door."

Exactly! When you close a sale, you shut off the competition; remove the prospect from the presence of other salesmen; close the door on them—and *you* pocket the commission.

Furthermore, any professional salesman will agree that the close *is* the sale. Whether he's in insurance, real estate or hospital supplies, he will agree that the close is the most important phase of the sales effort.

The salesman can arrange the interview, he can demonstrate the product, but those last few minutes when he actually goes for the close are the most critical. This is the point at which he will either get the sale or fall on his face, his time and effort wasted. This is when he needs some Big League Closing Techniques.

This book is going to show you how *not* to fall on your face; how to improve your closing percentage; to close from 16 to 17 out of 20 prospects.

Using specific techniques and true cases from my own experience and from hundreds of top producers—real pros—I have pinpointed the most effective, miracle closes; and you are going to see the *best* in action.

Whenever I found a majority of the high-board men agreeing on a specific approach to a closing problem—when they said, "Do it this way; it got me into the Big Leagues." I included it in this book, where it will also do the job for you.

This book will pinpoint your problems—they're basically the same in all fields of selling—*every one catalogued to place the most effective solutions* at your fingertips *where you can refer to them quickly and easily.*

Condensing all the words that have been said and printed about the close, you arrive at one basic question: Why does the prospect balk when he gets face-to-face with the decision to buy or not buy? You can call it sales resistance, you can call it reluctance to part with his money. You can say he wants to be sure he gets the best product, or the best price; or that he wants to be sure yours is the automobile or insurance program best suited to his needs.

But notice the bright-colored, basic thread of sameness woven into the pattern of all of the possible explanations for his balking at the close: Fear! Not the fear he would experience facing a loaded gun, but a fear almost as terrifying to him; the fear of making the wrong decision, of putting his signature to the contract; making that final, irrevocable move that ends the indecision right or wrong.

This being the case, what does he want? He wants to be reassured that there is nothing to fear; to go ahead; to be convinced; to get the agony of indecision over for once and for all.

This is where you, and this book, come in. In it you will learn to assist your prospect in overcoming that fear, that agony of indecision, by closing the sale—not after he has talked it over with his wife or colleagues, not after he's thought it over, not after he's seen your competition, but *now.*

These indecision-melters are more *effective—faster,* and *relatively effortless—*if you *follow them exactly as they're set down.*

Every plan or set of instructions must have a pattern. The pattern of this Big League how-to-close book will follow what I call the "Brick Overcoat" as its pattern or theme. Step-by-specific-step, it will remove the bricks until the prospective buyer is stripped of his fear—his sales resistance—and becomes susceptible to a close.

Once the bricks have been removed and neatly stacked on your or his desk—and here is the key—you will use them, *his own bricks,* to build a close, step-by-step; a close *so strong and convincing* that he will be *eager to sign.*

The "experts" have always told you that the sale is never made before the fourth or even the fifth contact; that a good salesman only closes three or four out of twenty possibles, and that "sales are in direct proportion to the number of prospects contacted."

Baloney! I can prove to you that this is simply not true. This book will show you that the sale should be and can be made at the *first* or *second* contact. You *should*, and you *will*, *close* rather than lose *16* to *17* out of every *20 bonafide, qualified prospects.*

One of the experts' claims is partially true: sales are directly proportional to contacts, but using this book you will be *selling*, not *interviewing* as many salesmen are now doing.

If you are tired of talking to dozens of prospects before you make a sale; if you want to learn how to remove the "Brick Overcoat" with a minimum of time and effort; if you want to learn to use the bricks from the overcoat to build a sale 75 percent of the time; if you want to earn top money and have time to play, then read and re-read this book. And keep it handy it's your Big League closing Bible.

--LES DANE

before the team, or even the bill, could it? But a good salesman only does. There is lots out of every possible, and that sales are in direct proportion to the number of prospects contacted.

balanced. I can prove to you that sales simply don't add up. But show you that the sale should be made to make it, at the part of every contact. You should, and you will more rather than lose 10 to 17 out of every 20 contacts and have no sales.

One of the most telling departmental true sales are directly proportional to prospects. Telling the people you will be walking, not interesting as many salesmen are now doing.

If you are tired of calling to dozens of prospects before you make a sale, if you want to learn how to remove the "Drop O should, with a minimum of time and effort, if you want to cut to cut the bricks to the eventual total and sell 75 percent of the time, if you want to earn top money, and have the freedom! Read and re-read this book until it becomes firmly ... your subconscious mind.

Table of Contents

9 The Four Basic Buyer Types: How to Close Them and Keep Them Closed 139

10 How to Prospect at the Close: Let the Customer Work for You 155

11 Five Big League Guidelines for Effective Paper Work: How They Can Help You at the Close 165

xii

1

The Brick Overcoat of
Resistance to the Sale:
How Five Key Bricks Can Help You

The prospective customer, when the time for his appointment with the salesman gets near, or he leaves the house to shop, wraps himself in a brick overcoat.

The coat is made up of all the arguments—concious or unconcious—the salesman must overcome to get the sale.

Much as a logger must locate and blast out the key pieces in a log-jam so the logs will break loose and continue their trip down river to the mill, so must the salesman locate the *key bricks* in the overcoat of sales resistance.

Once he has located those bricks it is a simple matter to remove them and move in for the Big League close.

There is one basic theme, however, which will appear throughout this book: fear. The bricks in the overcoat are bricks of *fear,* and fears must be dissolved so the prospect can move ahead with the purchase, confident that he is doing the right thing; getting the right product.

Can his fears—the bricks—be identified? Are they sticking out, a different color, size or shape than the rest of the coat? They are indeed. Sometimes the color is barely a shade different; the shape the tiniest fraction off. But if the salesman knows what to watch, and *listen* for, he can spot them every time.

Scaredy-Cat

The most oft-encountered key brick is the same size as the others, but the color is glaringly different. It stands out so glaringly that it might as well have a handle, waiting for you to seize it and pull it out. The prospect makes an obvious, futile effort to cover it with "but's" and "maybe's", but to the experienced closer the scaredy-cat is easy to handle.

"This looks like the car for me—I like the design and the color, but I think I'd better wait a few days. Maybe I won't like it after I've had it a while."

Or, "This portfolio of mutual funds you've prepared is exactly what I need and want, but maybe I'd better talk it over with my wife. After all, she'll be helping me make the payments, ha-ha."

Have you ever heard that before? Do you see the pattern? He's a *scaredy-cat* and he's one of the easiest, to sign up *because he doesn't have a legitimate reason for not going ahead.* The brick is there, but it's so obvious that he's stalling, looking for an excuse not to go ahead, that he makes it easy for you to pluck out the brick and hand him a pen, letting the overcoat crash in a shambles at his feet

The professional closer can shoot his arguments full of holes—*subtly* please—as fast as he can present them.

If he thinks he should show the portfolio of mutuals to his wife then why didn't he arrange for her to be present at the meeting? If he thinks he will get tired of the color, then isn't it entirely possible that he might get tired of *any* color he chooses?

He is faking! He's casting about for reasons not to buy, and this is where you move in for the close.

Take the "Maybe I'd better show it to my wife," gambit.

My answer would go in this direction:

"Mr. Peters, I can sympathize with your feeling that you ought to show it to your wife, especially in view of the fact that you told me she works too.

"But what does she know about the growth-potential of Power Nucleon? What does she understand about a plan offering 70 percent solid, slow-earning funds, 20 percent mildly spec investments, and the other 10 percent strictly wildcat stuff?

"Mr. Peters, you've shown me *you're* the man who's going to have to administer this fund—do the buying and selling—so why not give the madame a break and don't bother her with it, or embarrass her by pointing out the fact that she knows very little about it.

"Now. There is one important thing she might know about; the payment. It is within the figure you and she discussed, or did she, as most wives do, tell you to use your own good judgment?"

"Well, she did say to do it myself—that I know more about financing than she does. . . ."

"She knows her husband, Mr. Peters. She knows he is able to get the best for her and their little girl."

The fellow who's alibi is that the car (or whatever) might be the wrong color? He's easy, too. Here's one way:

"Mr. Peters, how long have you worked for Reminghouse Electric?"

"Fourteen years. I've been there since high school. Never had another job, except part-time while going to high school."

"I see. Married twelve years, I think you said. Smoked the same brand of pipe tobacco your whole life and driven this make of car for. . .you said you've had eight of them, I think.

"Mr. Peters, you are a careful person, and I admire you for it. But don't you see what I'm getting at? Your judgment has been nearly perfect your whole life. The right wife, the right tobacco, the right job, and the right car, except for the one time you tried another; and you came right back to this one.

"My point is that if you like this color now, your judgment will bear you out. And you've said your wife *likes* blue."

Field his argument and toss it right back—*gently*, now—at him. Mixed with a bit of simple, honest flattery, it will wrap him up better than 90 percent of the time.

In any case, *don't overdo it.* If you've labeled him wrong, and his *is* a legitimate, heart-felt alibi, you'll wind up with egg on your face, and a lost sale.

Suggest that his wife is a scatter-brain who wouldn't know a mutual fund from a roller-coaster ride and he'll tell you that she works at a computer factory, running final test on their product.

Tell him it would be impossible for an intellectual giant like him to make a mistake and he'll tell you about the time that he put a down-payment on a deal to buy forty acres of the parking lot at the Astrodome.

Find the key brick—the *alibi*. Once you've decided he's simply a scaredy-cat, remove the brick and use it to close the deal.

Practice will show you how to spot this type. He will be fine right up to the close. He'll agree with everything until you say,

"Let's go in the office," or, "Sign here." Then he'll begin to search for reasons not to buy.

He's been busy getting sold, and all of a sudden realizes that if he doesn't move fast, doesn't come up with a quick alibi, he's gone. This is where he tosses out the first one that comes to mind, and you can spot it as just that; not a bona-fide reason for waiting or not buying, but a scaredy-cat's desperate effort to keep from signing when he *knows* he *wants to*.

The Legitimate Objection

The next brick is not as easy to handle. In this case, the prospect tells you his objection, but presents two problems in removing the brick.

First, he comes up with what seems to be a perfectly legitimate reason for waiting. You try, but discover that this is *not* the scaredy-cat type; that he has a real need to wait, or at least a bona-fide reason for *thinking* he has.

No matter how hard you try, you can't get the brick out! You've found it, but it is so firmly wedged in the coat you can feel him slipping away.

These are two *distinct* and *separate* problems, and must be *dealt with separately*. Let's look at the difference between the scaredy-cat alibi and the legitimate one. How do you spot the real objection?

The most obvious indication that the prospect has what he feels is a legitimate reason for waiting or not buying is that he sticks to that *one objection*.

Rather than come up with a new one each time the salesman tries to overcome it, he repeatedly goes back to the *same argument*. He is sincere, and firmly believes that his objection is a valid one—which it well might be.

Another good indication of a valid alibi is an objection that makes sense, or has a ring of authenticity to it rather than the ridiculous objections of the scaredy-cat.

A third sign that the salesman is going to have his work cut out for him is the case of a man and his wife, two or more partners, or a group where they all have to agree to the purchase.

If all of those concerned are in agreement that they should wait, shop around, or not buy at all, then the salesman can assume that they have produced a valid argument against the transaction, making his job harder, but not impossible.

We've seen how to handle the scaredy-cat, but how do we approach the legitimate objection?

Listen For the Close

I recall a sale I made a few years ago that I felt was lost—at least for six months—which was the basis of my prospect's objection.

He had contacted the agency I was selling for and told the sales manager he was going to be in the market for a fleet of pickups (five) and a big job in *six months.*

He operated a small garage up town, so I drove over to see him. He was a young fellow, in his early thirties, and from the appearance of his shop and equipment seemed to have a modest but active business.

We talked about the trucks, and he made it clear that he would not be in a position to buy for at least six months. He had applied to a federal agency that makes secured loans to small businesses for a loan to start a welding operation. They had told him that his application looked good, but that the paper work could take as much as half-a-year to complete. Knowing how government agencies operated, I believed it, and felt that he had a legitimate reason not to go ahead. In fact he *couldn't* go ahead.

Or could he? I let him talk. The salesman who runs into a snag in the initial phase of the selling operation should *listen, not talk.* It often happens that the prospect will suggest a way to get around his own objection, provided he is a bona-fide prospect.

This man had a sound idea that he wanted to get started. He was going to mount portable welding machines in the pickup, so that he could go anywhere, and then use the big truck as a backup to carry spare parts, equipment, and supplies. He had a background in welding and mechanical repairs of everything from machinery to appliances, and had already lined up some steady, reliable men who were anxious to come in with him.

I learned this by *listening,* gently prodding him with a question here and a suggestion there, but essentially *letting him do the talking.* Then I had an idea.

"Mr. Porter, do you have a copy of your financial statement and the other papers necessary for your loan application at the federal agency?"

"Right here in the office." He opened a desk drawer and handed me a manila folder with copies of the proposed transaction.

"If I can get the money you need at the same or better terms, can you see your way clear to go ahead, understanding that you need not use my idea unless your attorney says you should?"

"Well, I wanted to work through the federal loan agency, but if they're going to be so long and you think you might arrange it, yes, I'd go ahead. This is an idea I believe in, and I want to get started. If it works out I'll give you the order for the trucks soon as I have the money."

I called my bank from the man's office, told the loan officer I had a good loan prospect for him, and made an appointment.

"Mr. Dane, that bank turned me down. They said my collateral wasn't sufficient to cover the purchase of rolling stock, it being subject to breakdown and damage. I didn't talk to your man, but they turned me down."

"Mr. Porter, this man knows me, and he knows I wouldn't try to sell him a con job. He wouldn't buy one anyway, but let me talk to him, and show him my idea. Nothing ventured, you know."

That night I studied the pamphlet that the federal people issue to loan prospects and found what I had suspected: some banks "participate" in these loans, where the bank guarantees half the money and the government the other half.

The next day Porter and I kept the appointment with the banker, and, armed with the letter from the local federal office, presented my proposal.

The government loan application would be allowed to go through. In the meantime the bank would put up the necessary money for Porter to get started.

They would take the collateral as security and would then decide at the approval of the loan by the federal people whether they wanted out, or if they wanted to participate. The plan was approved in ten minutes.

They did the paper work, and in a week Porter had his money. Had the federal people turned the loan down, Porter would have had to make payments to the bank twice as high as theirs, because the bank could only give him 30 months while the government loan would be for five years. But they approved the loan and Porter was in the welding business.

I got the order for the trucks and recommended a supplier for the welders and equipment he needed. I also got a fat commission from the welding supplier, because after all, it isn't every day they sell five welding machines and the equipment necessary to operate them.

As I've said, the key to removing the brick here was *listening*, getting the whole story, and then letting the prospect talk himself into a "go" position—with a little help from me.

There is another good point to remember here: cultivate the finance men. Show them that you are an honest, legitimate salesman. Take your prospects to them when you hit a money snag and watch them go.

Whether savings and loan, finance company, or bank, they'll make every effort in their power to make the loan, and you'll get the sale. We'll discuss this in more detail later in the chapter.

I handle the more-than-one legitimate objection in much the same way, but my experience has been that it is even simpler. Let them talk, with you sitting on the sidelines throwing out a suggestion here, a hint there—all aimed at removal of the key brick that will get you the close.

Thus the way to approach the person with a legitimate objection or reason for hesitating is to listen to the objection, encourage him to discuss it, and wait for him to overcome it himself.

Failing that, by *listening* you have gotten the whole background of his objection and should be able to come up with a suggestion that will eliminate the brick and prepare him for the close.

The Night Shift Close

A very successful insurance salesman friend of mine has been his general agent's training officer for ten years. He made the million dollar club for three consecutive years, and the men he's training consistently produce high returns. I asked him about the "brick overcoat."

"Sales resistance—the 'brick overcoat' as you put it—is the one reason we need salesmen. If it weren't for sales resistance there would be no need for them.

"I try to get it across to a new man right from the first day that once he has determined the need for insurance and the ability to buy on his prospect's part, he is ready to move for the close.

"The next, and most important point I make is that they must go to the client, not make the client come to them. And I don't mean at their office, their place of business, or the corner saloon. My favorite sales talk is titled "Work the Night Shift," and that's exactly what I teach my men to do.

"I learned from the first few months I was in the insurance business that I am like the doctor, dentist, or analyzer. I am a professional, and I am asking for the privilege of becoming involved in my prospect's most intimate personal life.

"I saw that appointments at his office, where he had business on his mind, constant interruptions from his secretary, and telephone calls, were not paying off.

"I saw that because he was a busy man, he didn't have time to come to my office either, and when he did he was ill at ease, and not ready to be sold.

"What was the answer? Work at night. I started leaving the house about noon or one o'clock, and working the hardest *after supper.*

"Arriving at the office in the early afternoon gave me plenty of time to do my paper work, catch up with my correspondence, and make the evening's appointments.

"A typical appointment call would sound something like this: 'Mr. Smith, this is Jim Bagley, at Southwestern Life. How are you? Been fishing lately? (Here, knowing your prospect helps, but *don't* take up his whole afternoon.)

'I thought that if you were going to be in this evening, I'd come over for a few minutes. I have something you need to see. Would eight be best, or would you rather I came earlier? I'll be available, let's see, from six-thirty on.' (Notice the choice, making it difficult to say "no.")

'Fine. I'll see you about seven then.'

"Not a long call taking up his whole day. A comment that showed I *knew* the man I was calling, and had something for him, without tipping my hand on the telephone where it couldn't, and *wouldn't* end in a sale.

"Why work at night, at the prospect's home? Several good valid reasons are clear if you look at it carefully.

"As I've said, you are asking to involve yourself in his private life, his *personal business.* What better place than in *his home* where he feels *relaxed* and *comfortable?*

"Another reason is his *wife.* Who is going to benefit more from the insurance I'm trying to sell than his wife and children?

"The same applies if he outlives the policy. I have closed many a policy or insurance plan with the comment, as I stood looking out into his back yard, 'I can just see you and your wife sitting by your swimming pool, your grandchildren frolicking in the water.'

"I want the family—the wife anyway—there so that I can answer all the questions understandably. Too many sales are lost because the *wife wasn't considered,* or because she asked questions which the prospect couldn't answer. I've had an argument develop and the sale

go down the drain when the husband said, 'All right! I won't buy *any* insurance if you don't trust my judgment.' Well, whether *she* does or not, *I* don't trust his judgment until he's *signed up.*

"I realize that this method, this night-shift selling, might not apply to all fields, but I would think that even in hard goods, furniture, or anything else, the close would be simpler and easier at the prospect's home.

"I'd stake my life on the fact that this is true where the wife has an interest in the purchase, like a car, a home, furniture, insurance, investments, savings program, cemetery plots, or even magazine subscriptions.

"Those key bricks in the overcoat will fall away a lot faster and easier if you can approach the prospect in the 'safety' of his own home where he feels secure and familiar.

"And one more thing," he laughed, "he can't tell you that he wants to talk it over with his wife!"

Laughing or not, that last statement is pertinent and true. Not only have you robbed him of the chance of saying that, but you are there to explain what you're trying to sell, and you might wind up with a very powerful ally, his wife, in your closing approach.

You and the Finance Man

I touched earlier upon the financing aspect of the close, but in a different manner. There, the trip to the bank was to get rid of the, "I-have-to-wait" brick. But financing, or the lack of it, has lost many sales for many salesmen; ones that should have been closed.

When I tell them that a knowledge of financing, properly applied, can help with the close, most salesmen react typically.

"I have to do the selling. Why the financing too? After all, I'm a salesman, not a loan officer."

Anything Goes

I say that the man who takes this attitude is *not* a salesman. He only *thinks* he's one.

I say that *anything you can do* to enable you to get the close *faster* and *easier*, so you can turn your attention to the next prospect, is *part of salesmanship.*

I've fixed the baby's formula while the parents discussed my offer. I've washed a car that the service department overlooked with the customer on the way to pick it up. I've even loaned a prospect $100 because he wanted the boat rig I was trying to sell him and didn't have any money with which to put up a deposit.

Whatever it is, if it brings me and my prospect closer to the dotted line, then it is a part of the *every-day selling job* that feeds me and my family.

Getting back to financing; experience and talks with other successful producers has shown that the reply to the question, "What happened?" when a prospect gets away is very often, "I couldn't get him the necessary financing."

Discussions with sales managers and top men show that a follow-up of this question and its attendant answer show that *more than half* of those lost could have been salvaged by applying a *working knowledge* of *financing procedures.*

"It's nice, but I can't afford it right now."

"I know I need more insurance, but I have so many payments now. . ."

"I've already been to the bank, and they won't give me any more. . ."

You hear these objections every day, and the "salesmen" who says, "Well, if that's the case, it's been nice talking to you, Mr. Jones, but I don't see how I can. . ." is not a salesman, but a sure-thing artist, an order-taker.

When the going gets tough, when he has to *dig for the close,* he loses interest. But he has forgotten one major point: he has *qualified* this person as a *buyer,* and *there's a way* for him to get the close.

I don't mean a way to deceive the prospect and/or the finance officer. I mean a *legitimate approach* to the purchase he needs or wants to make that will satisfy all concerned.

Fool-Proof Financing Formula

A question asked casually at a lunch date with a local bank's installment loan officer gave me a foolproof formula for saving deals that I had lost in the past.

"Jenks, you folks want to make the loan wherever possible because that's your business. Do you have a formula or plan you apply when a man asks for a loan, or do you have to approach the thing hit-or-miss, relying on experience and judgment, hoping you were right in accepting or rejecting the application?

"Years ago a man who he became the company president and retired a few years ago with more than 60 years in lending, showed me a simple formula that applied then and still applies.

"For example, let's say the customer is what we call 'good pay.' This means he has been doing business with us, has at least two paid-up contracts, and although he may have called us to say he would be late a time or two, had no real problem with his accounts.

"He makes $600 a month, take home, and wants to buy a boat rig that costs $3000. He wants to keep the payment fairly low, say $85 monthly, or less. He has told me that he realizes he can't handle any more than that.

"Here's the formula: his shelter, whether he rents, is buying, or owns his house clear, *could take one week's pay,* or $150. His transportation, car, car pool, rental car, or bus, another week's pay; *no more.* Groceries, a full week's pay for the month. Again, *no more* than that.

"We have used three-quarters of his take-home pay. But we have to keep the miscellaneous and incidentals in mind. The things that crop up unexpectedly; a broken arm, a set of tires for the car, a new washer, insurance, clothes, etc.

"These account for the last quarter. Now we get to *the key to the formula:* instead of dividing the four-week month by *four,* we go a step further in being careful not to burden our man and *divide by five."*

At this point I was busily taking notes on a paper napkin, sure that he was giving me a valuable lesson in economics and financing.

"Dividing by five gives him an extra margin of safety, so now we list his payments, bills, and obligations to the nearest dollar. In other words, we don't round an $18 payment off to $20, or $15. We list it as *$18.*

"Here's how it would work: Our man who wants a boat pays $105.54 for his house payment, including insurance, full coverage, which would at least replace the home in the event of total loss. This becomes *$106.*

"His car payment on a new car bought last year is $89.26. *$89.* Groceries, on which he gets a break because he has only one small child $35 a week, or *$140 a month.* Miscellaneous remains at *$150* for now because that can't be pinned down, and we must keep the safeguard in mind.

"He has other installment loans in the amount of $67.78, or $68, making total accountable bills $553 a month, leaving $47 clear, after *all* possibilities have been covered and a built-in safeguard provided.

"Now let's go back to the division by five. This would allow $125 for the house—he was $19 *low.* Car, $36 *low,* and he has a year's equity. This payment will be gone one year before he pays for the rig. Groceries, he was $10 *low,* and of course miscellaneous is now on the money at $125.

"Let's analyze it now, and see what he can do *safely.* He has a spendable excess of $47, a car one-third paid for that should last at least seven more years, and $71 in payments that will pay out during the next two to three years.

"This man can pay $90 per month easily, and would not be in danger at $100. With the $500 down payment he must have anyway he can buy the boat and *enjoy owning* and running it. Of course it also holds true that when he has gotten to the half-way point he will be in excellent position to obtain relief if he wants or needs to. He didn't *know* he could do it!"

I have used this formula dozens of times in overcoming the objection, believed and honestly felt by my prospect, that, "I want it, but I can't afford the payment."

Eliminate the financing objection with the honest and accurate application of this formula, but a word of caution: when it shows that the prospect can't afford it, *tell him so*. When he *can* afford it he'll come to you. That too, has happened to me, and I know it has happened to you. Why? Trust.

The Shopper-Stopper

The shopper is the one that taxes my ability more than any other. This guy can be absolutely *determined* not to take my word for it that I have the best he can buy.

But I have found the way to handle even this tough nut. Again, I asked salesmen of all types how they overcome the "I want to look around" objection, and then boiled their answers down to three proven "Shopper-Stoppers."

The Go-Ahead

I call my first shopper-stopper "The Go-Ahead."

This technique will not get the close right then; that is, in most cases, but it *will* insure that you get another shot at the prospect's business.

In this shopper-stopper I use some left-handed psychology. I plant a carefully fertilized seed of doubt and turn the prospect loose to do all the shopping he wants to, with the admonition to come back with all the facts and figures *when he's completed his shopping.*

Here you must qualify the prospect very carefully. You need to be a *real judge of people* and what makes them tick. The only one susceptible to the go ahead approach to the close is the person who is *definitely* and *irrevocably determined*, no matter what you say or do, to shop. This is whether he's looking at an automobile, an insurance policy, or $100,000 worth of chemicals for his plant.

Here's how it works:

He has made it clear that he's going to shop, no matter what. So you take out insurance that he'll be back. Don't give him a firm figure on the price for which you will deliver the chemicals.

Simply tell him that you know you can beat the lowest figure available for chemicals of the specifications he needs, and that *nobody can beat your figures or specs.*

Then you tell him that you admire his determination to get the best at the lowest figure. After all, you, a trained salesman, always do exactly the same thing.

"Mr. Jones, good for you. You operate just like I do. After all, this is *your money* you're getting ready to spend, and believe me, if it comes as hard to you as it does to me, you'd *better* look around.

"Now, I know you can't do better anywhere else, and you'll help me get the sale if you'll look around and convince *yourself.* When you've finished, bring the facts and figures to me and I'll prove to you that mine is, after all, the best deal for you. O.K.?"

He *has* to come back. You have talked in generalities, not firm facts or figures, so you get the last shot at his business without committing yourself.

"That isn't fair. You give me *your* figures, and if you're low I'll be back. If not, I'm buying from the lowest I can find."

"I'm sorry, Mr. Jones, but I can't do that. There are a lot of things to be considered in a purchase of $100,000 worth of chemicals, and I'm not going to let you make a mistake if I can help it. I am a professional salesman, and I owe it to you to be precise. You see the others and then I'll go over the whole deal with you."

You will lose a few of these, but there's no way to get them anyway. They are determined to get the lowest figure, and that's *all* they consider.

Most of them won't be able to resist the "I'll-show-you-when-you-come-back-that-mine-is-the-best-deal-and-they-can't-beat-it" offer.

Suppose, you say, that he has a bona-fide offer from another supplier, at a lower price than you can come to.

Remember: you did not say the lowest *price.* You said *the best deal.* You said the *best chemicals* for the *least money.*

When he contacts you again, whether he's coming to your office or you're going to him, you have two things going for you. He has heard so many specs, prices and details of the deals the competition has, that he's confused and tired. He wants to get it over. In other words, your competition has *prepared him* for a *close.*

The other point you've gained is that now you can pick the

other deal to pieces while the competition is not there to defend himself. You can attack *delivery dates*; your chemicals are three percent stronger according to government tests and you have the full supply in your warehouse *now*—no ordering and waiting for delivery.

Even if your price *is* a bit higher, you can sell him, because now you have the opposition, the real objection, *out in the open* where you can wrestle with it.

A good salesman can throw this "objection" five falls out of six.

The Today-Only Close

I call the next shopper-stopper "Today Only."

You see ads every day in the papers, for a number six can of orange juice or an average three-pound roast of beef at such-and-such a price *today-only.* In other words, if I don't get the business today I can't promise, and there's the key, *promise,* to give you the same deal tomorrow or Saturday. Why?

Use your imagination. Today is the last day of a sales contest, or today is the last day for you to qualify for the million-dollar club and you're close, or simply the company always goes rock-bottom at the end of the year or month.

"Mr. Jones, you've told me that you need these ballpoint pens, and that they have been the best advertising gimmick you've found."

"That's true all right, but I want to check with Acme Advertising. They called the other day and told me they wanted a crack at my business, and you can't blame me for. . ."

"Of course not, Mr. Jones. I don't blame you one bit. All right. You are determined to check with them, so I'll have to give you a reason to go ahead and give me the order now.

"I lack about three hundred dollars of earning a bonus as top man for the month. Now, don't get the wrong idea. I don't expect you to help me win a bonus. But I *will* call my sales manager and get you a price that will show you that *today only* you can buy these pens for. . .

"You understand, of course, that I might not always be able to deliver them at this price Mr. Jones; just today."

If it's a large item, one of unusual color, or a special price he's interested in, it then becomes the "last one, and two other salesmen have people looking at it. I sure hope you don't leave and then find it gone when you get back. The madame, ha-ha, would surely be disappointed.

"She did say that it was her only color choice, eh, Mr. Jones?"

You can improvise and come up with many, many more Today-Only shopper-stoppers, geared to the product or service you're selling.

Simple Sell Close

This last shopper-stopper is titled the *Simple Sell* approach.

The simple sell is exactly that. No tricks, no gimmicks, just a straightforward, simple, "Why not go ahead with this car or this plan or this policy now?

"Mr. Jones, you and your wife have told me that you want to see the dealer down the street before you buy. I can understand that you want the best, and I'm certainly not knocking him, but look at it this way.

"We've been right here on this same property for years, and our business has multiplied five times. We have customers who come to us year in and year out, and even bring their children when they're ready.

"Mrs. Jones likes this one, too. She likes the color and the design, don't you, Mrs. Jones? Well, why not go ahead," you look at your watch, "and let me get it ready? You can be home in time for supper and catch your favorite television show, knowing that the agony of having to shop is over."

Simple. Direct. Not overdone. A subtle appeal for help from the wife. Hit the target with both barrels, and watch how simple it can be to wrap the sale up, *then* and *there.*

The beauty part of this shopper-stopper is that you'll still have the other two to use if it fails. But you won't usually need them.

2

The Big League Go-Button
for the Close:
How to Find It and
When to Push It

In Chapter 1 we discussed the brick overcoat of sales resistance and how to locate and remove the key bricks to prepare the prospect for the close.

Finding those bricks and getting them out of the way is important, but it is not, by any stretch of the imagination, the whole story of a successful close. It is really the *beginning* of the end; the beginning of the *close*. There is one more very critical—perhaps more critical—phase which must be handled, and handled carefully, or all the work that has gone before might be wasted.

The Gladiators

We saw in Chapter 1 that the prospect puts on his brick overcoat when he leaves the house to shop for the car, power mower or mutual fund portfolio of his choice. When the situation is reversed and you have an appointment to see him in his office, he dons it a few minutes before you arrive.

So that we can see the salesman and the prospect in their proper perspective, let us picture them as two Roman gladiators of many years ago. Each has his armor and his double-edged sword. The battle (sales approach) begins.

The fight see-saws back and forth. The prospect raises his sword and slashes at the salesman (objection). The salesman sidesteps (fields the objection) and thrusts with his sword (tossing the objection back as a reason to buy).

And so the battle (sales approach) goes until the salesman sees an opening. Quick as a flash he hooks the clasp of the prospect's armor and it falls to his feet (objection gone, brick removed). The prospect stands defenseless, his armor gone, susceptible to a carefully aimed thrust (the close).

In Roman times the gladiator would have stepped forward and mercilessly driven his sword to the hilt in the breast of his adversary, but this is where the comparison between the Roman gladiators and a salesman with his prospect ends.

Thrust now and the salesman may be the one who dies (no sale, the close lost).

It is true that the prospect has lost his armor. His brick overcoat lies shattered at his feet. He stands helpless, with no weapon with which to fight back. Or does he?

Put yourself in his shoes for a moment. He unconsciously encased himself in the overcoat of sales resistance, knowing he was safe from the attacks of the salesman.

Then, quite suddenly, he finds himself naked and vulnerable. But is he helpless? Vunerable, *yes,* helpless, *no.*

He can say "no." This may be the most critical few seconds or minutes in the closing process. He can still say "no," and will, unless handled very carefully from this point to the close.

In essence he's been defeated. Every objection he has offered in his defense has been torn away, and he feels beaten. Nobody enjoys the taste of defeat, so will cast around for anything to save the day, and in his case he has his one word that will undo all you have accomplished. The word is "no." By removing the bricks and ripping his armor aside, you have not won the fight; not by a jugful, for now you must locate the Go-Button and keep him from uttering that fateful word.

Find the Big League Go-Button

Just what is the go-button? It is a face-saver. The prospect, again unconsciously, was saying to himself, "This guy might think I'm a soft sell, a pushover, but I'll show him. I'll buy *what* I want *when* I'm ready, and not a *minute before.*"

Now that you have robbed him of his armor and made him vulnerable to a close, make him like it. Make it sound as if he meant to be closed all along. Why? For two reasons: first, he saves face—the purchase becomes *his* idea, *his* decision again, which after all it *is* and second his *unconscious resistance* to the close becomes a *conscious desire to buy.*

Locating the Big League Go-Button will be as different with every prospect as his personality, his home life, his job, physical appearance, and everything else that makes him a distinct person.

A Lesson in Applied Psychology

I knew when Jim started with us that he was going to be a good man. He was likeable, good-looking, and had a great deal of personality. He was persuasive, neat, and a good talker. In short, a born salesman. And he loved to sell. He was also six-foot four and weighed a muscular 285 pounds.

Yet he fell flat on his face. Seven, eight, even nine out of ten prospects would get away in spite of his being one of the most accomplished brick-removers I had ever worked with.

I was a closer for the agency, and had had occasion to see Jim in operation many times. His approach was good, and he varied his sales talks, matching them to the prospect. His qualifying was faultless.

And yet time after time he would lose out at the close—fail to find the go-button. Naturally, this got to his pride as a professional and I could see a good man going into some other line of work, defeated by a simple flaw which took me a month of watching to find.

Jim was *too enthusiastic.* Not too eager—too enthusiastic. You wonder how he could be *too* enthusiastic, assuming that enthusiasm was a prime requirement of successful selling, right? Not always. Not this kind, anyway.

With Jim's approval I had bugged his office and listened as he handled a close. Everything would be fine right up to the last point—finding and pressing the go-button. Then he'd blow it.

But how? There was nothing in his speech or attitude that I

could put my finger on. As I listened he would become enthusiastic, sure, but at the right time, and I would be sure he had the sale, only to see the prospect leave or hear Jim call for a closer. Why?!

I decided it had to be something he was *doing,* not what he was *saying* that was losing so many good, sound deals for him. I asked him to move out of his closing office and into the showroom where I could loiter around and watch him, in addition to listening to his close approach.

Then, one day when he had a very short, thin fellow, about five feet even, and 125 pounds—I saw the trouble. He was *badgering his prospects* without even realizing it. He was badgering them with his *size and enthusiasm.*

Jim sat at his desk, the prospect facing him from another chair. When he arrived at the go-button point Jim jumped up and alternately sat on the edge of the desk close to the prospect or leaned on the desk over him. The little fellow was *terrified* of the big galoot!

The solution was simple. I went over to them, excused myself, and told Jim I needed to borrow a chair. He looked like he thought I had lost my mind, but offered me his swivel chair.

His prospect's reaction proved I was on the right track. He jumped up, offered me *his* chair and said, "Here, take this one. I'm tired of sitting, anyway."

What he meant was, "I'm tired of this giant looming over me, reminding me that I'm a little runt. But one thing is for sure; I don't *have* to buy from him, the big lug."

"Jim, would you mind bringing the chair in my office for me. My old back is acting up again."

He knew there was nothing wrong with my back, but he got my message and followed me with the chair. In my office I gave him a rapid rundown of my theory.

"Jim, when you go back out there, don't offer him your chair. Get in it and *stay* in it *no matter what.* If he wants to sit on the floor, all right, but *don't* let him get into a chair. In fact, if I have it figured right he *won't want to.* Now, go get your close, and remember: *he* stays on his feet, *you* stay in the *chair.*"

It was beautiful to watch. The little guy turned the tables on Jim. He hovered over him, leaned on the desk, and thoroughly enjoyed himself—even while he was signing the contract.

The go-button? Realizing that this fellow was conscious of his size, or rather the lack of it, and envious of Jim's height and manly physique.

It developed that even with people of normal size Jim was letting his size and enthusiasm, which is usually an asset, work against him. When he got near the close point and went for the go-button an over-abundance of enthusiasm was causing him to "lean" on his prospect, and even an average-sized person, or one as big as Jim, felt cowed when he jumped out of his chair and hovered over him. They got even the only way they could—by saying "no."

The solution? Simple: stay in your chair; encourage the customer to be "bigger" or taller than you.

"Stay in your chair" has many applications which simply mean *adjust yourself to the prospect.* Certainly it applies throughout the sales approach, but never as much as it does when you're reaching for the go-button.

Remember, during the approach the prospect still has his armor, is still feeling safe from your attack. But when you've overcome his resistance, things change. Now he's going to resort to his one remaining weapon, "no," and he is going to be casting around for reasons, since you've robbed him of those he brought with him, to reject you. Don't give the reasons right back to him in the form of your own failure to locate the go-button, by not adjusting your personality to fit his.

Slap His face

When I had been in sales a very short time I learned a lesson from a sales manager, one that has served me all through the years. I call it "Slap His Face."

I pride myself on being a neat and orderly person. Things out of place in my home, office, or car make me nervous until they're back where they belong.

This habit of order and neatness very nearly cost me the first selling job I ever had.

It was a part-time job in the J.C. Penny Company store in Niagara Falls, and I was on a small salary plus commission. I sold in the men's department—suits, clothing, underwear, work clothes, even shoes—if it had to do with men's apparel, it was my department.

I kept it neat. I never let a suit lie on the counter any longer than it took the customer to leave the store. My shelves of underwear, shirts, and socks were orderly, and my shoe boxes were right-side up and flush with the front of the rack.

But I didn't sell much. On a commission of one dollar per hundred, I needed to sell, even in those days of lower prices, because a good suit was only $40, and a set of work clothes about $5.

One day the manager told the assistant that he liked me, but that I wasn't selling, and he guessed he'd have to let me go. We were enjoying good traffic, but my department wasn't moving the merchandise.

They talked it over, and the assistant, a fellow named Oliver, asked the manager to give him three days to get me selling or he'd fire me himself.

I had noticed—in fact it was the one thing I hated about my job—that every afternoon when I came to work my department was a mess.

Oliver worked there until I arrived in the afternoon from school, and it always took me an hour to put the suits, shoes, and things back where they belonged.

One day when I started to clean, up Oliver came over and said, "Leave it. I want to talk to you."

We went into the shoe section and sat down. I knew what was coming, for I knew my department wasn't getting its share of sales, even though I had figured every way I knew to get it going. I also knew Oliver did fine until I got there and took over, making the fault very clearly mine. Also, I was taking over in the evening, a time when the customer traffic was the heaviest, so sales should have been, too.

"Kid, the next time a customer walks into your department and takes a suit off the rack or musses up a stack of shirts, I want you to slap his mouth. *Hard.*"

I was dumfounded. He wasn't the type to kid around—always serious and businesslike.

"I don't understand, Mr. Oliver. You must be. . ."

"I am *not kidding.* You spend most of your time keeping your department neat and orderly, and who is a mere *customer,* to come in and mess up the place just because he wants to spend his money with us?"

"I still don't get it. You mean. . ."

"A prospect wants to be *led;* guided to the sale, not hounded by a salesman who follows him putting the merchandise back as soon as he's looked at it.

"Let me show you something." We went into the work clothes section, where he acted as if he were a customer, browsing, taking work shirts out of the stack, and moving overalls around as if he were looking for his size.

I fought the temptation to follow him and put them back. Then he took me to the counter, which was clean and neat, without so much as a sales book or piece of paper in sight.

"When you bring a prospect into a neat, everything-in-place area like this to close a sale you *shock* him. When you follow him around, replacing everything that he takes out, you *shock* him. It would be less of a shock if you would simply slap him, hard, and then go ahead with the sale.

"Back when I was selling insurance, I learned to keep my papers, contracts, policies, and other things on my desk where the prospect could see them and touch them if he so desired. Then when it came time to talk turkey I wasn't reaching out of sight and producing something that might frighten him; something that would chill the buying attitude I had developed. Scaring him like that would have undone all that I had accomplished.

"When your prospect wants to look, *let him.* If you keep everything out of sight and simply try to *tell* him what it is, he's not going to believe you, or be as interested as he would if he discovered it for himself.

"When he shops for shoes or work clothes, encourage him to *look at them,* to *feel them.* While he is looking, you can show him the features that you want him to see, the features that will help you to convince him that yours is the right product."

From that day forward Oliver couldn't, or at least didn't, in a whole day, get the sales that I got in four hours in the afternoons; and often at the end of the week my department would be high in dollar volume for the entire store.

My department stayed cluttered, too. It looked *used,* and my customers felt at home, for they felt that they were in a store where they could look for the item they wanted or needed without a clerk hovering over them acting as if he had something to hide, or was afraid for them to see something.

Fred Shahid, one of the best salesmen I've ever worked with, told me he has actually seen a prospect ready for closing break out in a cold sweat when the salesman reached for a contract or buyer's order and placed it on an otherwise uncluttered desk.

Another successful colleague told me that he leaves a pad of orders and two or three contracts mixed up with advertising literature on his desk.

Then, when he's ready for the close he simply rummages around on the desk, saying, "Let's see, now. That order blank is right here somewhere. . ." very often finds that the prospect has it in his hand! No last minute chill there.

Identify

Webb was another good salesman who was selling furniture in a middle-class neighborhood in Virginia Beach when I met him. I was visiting a friend, the sales manager of the firm for which Webb worked.

Paul ran a good store and a good sales staff, catering to those in the six-to-ten thousand dollar income bracket, such as shipyard workers, blue-collar, civil service people, and the like.

When Paul introduced me to Webb, I was struck by his neatness as well as his precise, well-modulated voice. He wore a vest, steel-rimmed glasses, a conservative suit, and perfectly matched tie. He was the typical, well-dressed, well-groomed college professor-type.

I had forgotten about him until Paul remarked over lunch that he was going to have to let Webb go, and that he dreaded doing it because he felt that he could have been an outstanding producer.

"From what you've said it isn't liquor or anything like that, Paul, so what's Webb's trouble? Does he think he's too good for the likes of you and me?"

It's curious that you should say that," Paul replied. "Webb is a nice guy, and certainly doesn't think he's too good for us, but he just doesn't get the close. He seems to be fine until he gets to the end, and then he loses it, time and again.

"The thing I'm curious about is your asking whether he thinks he's too good to be one of us. You meant 'too good to be a salesman,' didn't you?"

"I'm not sure I know exactly what I meant. But I noticed that he talks like a college prof, and that he's obviously a reserved, dignified fellow with a better-than-average education and background. Why *is* he selling furniture, Paul?"

"He says he likes it. And obviously he does. He's the last man to go home at night, he's enthusiastic, and he tries very hard for the sale; perhaps too hard."

Paul and I went back to the showroom, and on the way I decided I had to try to help this fellow find out why he was missing the go-button—if he'd let me.

I struck up a conversation with him, and after ten minutes of talk and listening to the other salesmen tease him, which he took goodnaturedly, I thought I had the answer: he wasn't *identifying* with his prospects.

He was selling in a store that sold average-priced furniture to average families—working people who probably had high school educations or at the very best one year of college or trade school.

Yet his everyday conversation was liberally sprinkled with words like "tenacity," "ubiquitous," and comments like, "I find that a lost sale throws me into the deepest depression imaginable, yet no matter how I strive to apply the tested principles of salesmanship, I find myself, more often than not, on the receiving end of a polite rejection."

You or I would have said, "No matter how hard I try, I lose the sale, and it's damned discouraging."

I asked Paul if Webb and I could use his office for a few minutes. We went in and closed the door.

"Webb, do you want some good advice, or would you rather look for employment better suited to your personality?"

"If you consider it within your power to. . ."

"Listen, Webb. You're a nice guy, and you have a great deal going for you, like appearance and intelligence. Besides, Paul tells me that you know this business inside out.

"I think I've found your trouble. I wouldn't buy a coffee table from you, and I'll tell you *why*. When you talk, you lose me. Your manner and speech is on a level so far above mine that I can't *identify* with you.

"Let me put it this way: you aren't selling jewelry at Cartier's or Rolls-Royces on Park Avenue. You are a *furniture* salesman selling *average* merchandise to *average* people.

"You obviously aren't a snob, but you do give that *impression.* Now, I don't know what you do in your spare time, but I'll bet I can make an educated guess.

"You probably have a season ticket to the opera, and your favorite reading is Shakespeare or Chaucer. Your idea of an exciting day off is bird-watching or a trip to an art museum, followed by a gourmet dinner.

"This is fine, but you need to *come down* to where your *prospects are* when you're working. Be a two-hat man, to coin a phrase. Follow your own likes and pursuits when you're off, but put on your every-day, just-like-the-next-guy hat when you're working.

"Apply it to the closes you're losing; it doesn't make much difference while you're laying the groundwork, because your prospect still has his sales resistance to protect him. But when you strip him of that, he starts to look for something on which to blame the use of his only remaining weapon, the word 'no.'

"And you are providing your prospect with just the excuse he needs. 'This guy is a snob,' or, 'Who does Webb think he is, tossing those big words at me? I'll show him.'

"Try it, Webb, and see if your closes don't increase *because your prospect feels* that *you're like him*—a working stiff with whom he can *identify.*"

I got a card from him a few weeks later. "Dear Les, Am now leading the board and enjoying being a 'two-hat man.' I'm learning to 'identify' with my prospects, and the sales are coming much easier."

Here was the case of a man whose manner was incompatible with his prospects. He was an intellectual in speech and manner while his prospects, for the most part, were average, middle-class people who found it difficult, if not impossible, to relate to him and his sales approach.

By adjusting his own personality and wearing two hats, he was able to save his job and do well in a field he loved.

The salesman must not only convince the prospect that he should buy, but that he should buy *from him.* Then he must convince him that it was his own idea all along, not something he was talked or forced into by a persuasive salesman, even though that is exactly what happened, more often than not.

What a Beautiful Dress

Identifying with your customer goes deeper than the limited reference we made to Webb and his problem. I worked with seven other men on a sales force where we put "identification" to the ultimate test and proved that it pays off when practiced *constantly.*

We were on open floor—whoever got to the prospect first got the first shot at him; no "ups," or "taking turns."

After having worked together for six months a pattern began to develop that I found hard to ignore. For example, when one of us got on thin ice with a young single, or a young couple, we called on Nathan. Usually, with his help, we'd get the close.

When a woman or girl appeared and the salesman ran into trouble, it was Walt who got the nod. I got the businessmen, and the military people went to Bruce, a retired Navy chief.

Then I saw clearly what we were doing unconsciously. When we needed help we were calling in the one who would be most likely to *understand their objections,* and be able to *overcome them* easiest.

Nathan was a young, sports-car, weekends-at-the-beach-type, active young man.

Walt was a flatterer, a lady's man. He was married, a good, solid husband and father, and could handle the women, having them eating out of his hand in no time. When I said, "I like that hat, Mrs. Jones," she'd look at me as if I had pinched her, but when Walt said, "Mrs. Jones, where *do* you buy your clothes? If you don't mind I'd like to send my wife there. You always look so, modern," you could see them melt, their sales resistance and misgivings gone.

One elderly lady told me, "I love Mr. Walt. He always makes me feel like I'm the only woman in the world, the liar!"

I had a background in business and had been on my own for some ten years in that city, so I not only knew my way around in the business world, but also knew many of the men in top-level positions. Consequently, I got the businessmen.

See the pattern? We were not even aware that we were saying to ourselves, "I'll get Bruce to help me with this Navy couple—he's been in the Navy", or, "Les should be able to help me with this purchasing agent—might even know him."

Once the pattern had emerged to the extent where I could see and study it, "The Switch" was born. I went to the sales manager and outlined my idea.

The open floor would stay as it was. When the salesmen determined with what basic type he was dealing, he would invent an excuse to switch salesmen and ring in the one who matched the prospect. We even had two fellows who could pinch-hit as sports enthusiasts, flatterers, or what-have-you, doing a convincing job at all of them. Both of them later became successful closers.

The boss agreed to let us try the idea, provided we were all agreeable, reminding us that he wanted sales, and that he didn't much care about how we got them.

We talked it over among ourselves and decided to try it for three months, with the stipulation that any two men could terminate the setup. In that event, we would go back to the old approach.

The end of the third month saw the sales manager say something that to us was the ultimate in praise from a hard-driving producer.

"Fellows, your new plan has really paid off. Sales are more than double the best month we had had up to three months ago. All I can say is that when I walk into that showroom now, I'm sure glad I work here, the way you guys are waiting to pounce."

We were *identifying* with our prospects. It's true that we were taking extra advantage by assigning the salesman with a similar background, but it *can* be done by the individual.

Don't Concentrate On One Type

No salesman should ever make the mistake of concentrating on one type of prospect. That is a trap, pure and simple. He will, unconsciously or not, get to where that type is the *only* one he can close. His sales talks will become trite and stilted, his approach dull and matter-of-fact, and his sales will suffer.

But there is no reason why he shouldn't specialize. When I say "specialize," I mean in the broad sense. Many insurance agencies are good examples of the specialized fields of selling. Much as we did in "The Switch", insurance firms often assign inquiries and prospects to an individual salesman because his background matches or he has demonstrated a knack for, closing that type of prospect.

A friend of mine who has an extensive background in insurance recently switched to the mutual funds department of his firm. I asked him why, with his background, he had made such a move.

"It's simple," he said. "You know that I was born and raised in a farming community. There are dozens of truck-farming families in my home area, and it was natural for me to start my insurance-selling career in my own neighborhood. In fact, most salesmen, especially in insurance, do the same.

"I have pretty well sewed up the insurance business in the area, and have enjoyed getting the sons and daughters' business as they come of age, marry, and so forth. By changing to the investment branch, I opened a whole new market in the same area where I'm known and trusted as their insurance agent.

"I haven't lost the insurance business. I'm still licensed to sell insurance, and do when my clients need more. But I can also offer a more diversified method of securing their future through investments, and since I know what most of them can and can't do, it's a natural, especially in view of the fact that the large, virgin market for insurance there has all but petered out.

"I have already seen my next move, and that will be my last. When I've covered the mutuals prospects, keeping in mind that, just as in insurance, there will be young people coming along, I'll make that move. But I'll still be *identifying* with my own kind.

"Real estate. By the time I've drawn the cream off the investments market there as I have the insurance, I'll be getting along, and ready to slow down. I'll go into real estate right here in the same company, and be able to move more slowly and at the same time service my insurance and mutuals clients.

"Just remember one thing. I don't stay strictly in my own area. I get prospects by referral and by mail, and I work them just as I do my farmer neighbors. I know that I'd get into a rut and go stale if I tried to be *that* selective."

Here was a fellow who was specializing for his main income, and doing a good job of it, but at the same time keeping his eyes open for new business not only right in the same area but in others as well.

This, I decided, is a salesman who will never go stale, and more than that, will rarely miss the go-button because he is *identifying*, selling where he can sell the best; *among his own kind.*

It all boils down to a simple, two-step process that will show you the go-button and tell you when the time is right to press it for the close.

Step one: make your prospect feel at home. Make him see that

he is the *most important person in the world* to you at that moment;
that you are interested in *him* and *his needs,* and that you have *his*
best interests at heart.

   Step two: making him feel at home is not enough. You must
also show him, whether he is or not, that he is among his *own kind,*
that he is where he *belongs;* where he should do business now and in
the future. This you accomplish by *identifying* with him. Then the
close is as simple as pressing the Big League go-button.

3

The Tag-Team Close:
How to Tag and Retreat and
Who to Team With

The tag-team close is not to be confused with "The Switch", touched on in the last chapter. "The Switch" was applied immediately when the salesman had established the type of prospect he was dealing with. He had immediately called in the salesman, unbeknown to the prospect, who could best handle that prospect.

Remember the tag-team wrestlers you've seen in person or on television? One starts the match, and as he begins to get in trouble or to get tired he tags the other man, who then takes over. The team that can tag the most effectively and wear the other team down wins the fall and the match.

The tag-team close works the same way. One salesman starts the transaction, works the prospect a while, and then tags a closer, the sales manager or another salesman who will gradually wear the prospect down until the close comes easy.

The tag-team advantage lies in the fact that the prospect has no partner to tag, and must face the sales team alone, watching his sales resistance melting, the bricks falling away as he comes closer and closer to buying.

But how do you go about tagging? It is more involved than simply slapping the hand of your partner as the wrestlers do.

It must be done *carefully*, with *finesse* and *tact*, or the prospect could be offended, or so frightened that he can never be closed.

Five Types of Tag

Tagging methods can be divided into five categories. Each tag is employed in a different set of conditions, and the right tag can be half the battle.

Probably the most popular approach is the one that I call the "Horse's Mouth Tag." This is where you tag with the sales manager the Training Officer, or a closer; someone in authority, hence the Horse's Mouth title.

You have come to a point with the customer where you've made every concession possible as to price, delivery date, or whatever the hangup is, and you still haven't come up with a close that he'll accept.

Of course you knew from experience not to use all your ammunition; you've saved some for the manager or closer. But at this point you're convinced that the prospect needs to hear it from the boss, from authority, so that he can convince himself that what you've been telling him or what the closer is *going* to tell him, is the truth.

This is all well and good, but what do you *say* to the prospect? Surely not, "Mr. Jones, you obviously don't believe what I'm telling you, so I'll get the boss to tell you and then maybe you'll believe it."

If a salesman told *me* that, I'd jump on the defensive and he'd *never* close a sale to me. I'm sure most of your prospects would be the same.

You have to use tact; slip into the tag smoothly, with an absolute minimum of lost motion and delay or the close could be lost forever.

The Horse's Mouth Tag

The Horse's Mouth Tag is used when the prospect has said, "I'll go ahead and sign today if you'll. . ." but his requirement is beyond your authority to grant.

Or he says he'll sign if your promise delivery by such-and-such a date, and you feel you can't deliver, or you don't *know* whether you can.

You tag the man higher in authority when you reach a point where you can't make the commitment or the decision.

Try not to leave the prospect. If you excuse yourself to look for someone higher up, it is going to require a discussion, a fill-in on the deal thus far, which takes time. And while you and the manager or T.O. are discussing the deal, your prospect is retrieving the bricks you've removed. You might have the whole job to do again! That is, if it isn't already too late when you get back.

One successful sales manager I know has a standing rule that he will help with a close only *in his office*. Why? So he can play the big-shot? Because he's lazy?

Because when you need the assistance of *authority* you need it where its *weight* and *prestige* can *be felt the most*. Take your prospect to the boss. Introduce him and then describe the problem. Let your T.O. or manager exercise his authority where it will have the utmost effect—from behind his *own desk*, in his *own office*.

When you decide to go higher for assistance, *don't* suggest it to the prospect. When you say, "Mr. Jones, I don't know whether we can promise delivery of that much steel in 60 days. Let's go talk to the manager and see what he says," you are, in effect, giving him an out.

He can simply reply, "You talk to him and then call me," or, "I don't want to put him to all that trouble. I'll just wait until another time."

A much better approach would be, "Wait. I have an idea. Come with me, Mr. Jones, and I'll get this thing straight right now."

Then walk out, leaving the door open. He'll follow because he's polite. He may not *want* to, but he will. *Don't* stop, *don't* slow down. Go straight to the man from whom you're going to seek help and let him take it from there.

If you're in the prospect's office and you're telephoning for help, don't suggest it. Ask to use the phone, dial your man, explain the problem briefly to him, and hand Mr. Jones the phone. He'll take it, again because he doesn't want to be rude or impolite.

There is another set of circumstances where the higher echelon can help you with a close, but it is even *more* up to you to recognize the conditions and *admit* you *can't handle it alone*.

Every salesman knows there are new, never-before-seen circumstances that can stop a close cold. These are things that you have never encountered before, that with all your years of experience you are not equipped to cope with.

First, admit that you're out of gas. Don't sit there cranking a dead engine. You'll probably do more harm than good, and at best you'll accomplish *nothing.*

Second, tag the next higher man. He is higher than you due to outstanding ability, more experience, or both. He may have encountered the same problem before—remember, as manager or T.O. he deals with the salesmen's problems every day—and may have the solution at his fingertips. If he hasn't seen it before, he may have the *ability* to see the solution from experience or simply because so often an outside observer can see something you can't.

And even if he got his job by marrying the boss' daughter he has a powerful weapon you don't have: *authority.*

We'll Build It or We'll Go Broke Trying

There's a story that was printed in trade papers all over the country that illustrates the Horse's Mouth Tag perfectly. It also points up the necessity of tagging the *right partner.*

Greg represents one of the largest and most successful industrial building contractors in the area. Two men started the firm ten years ago with a pickup truck and two sets of carpenter tools, and today are worth several million dollars.

Greg had watched the papers, waiting for a large aircraft engine manufacturing plant to announce that it had decided to exercise its option and build an engine-assembly plant here. When the announcement came, he called their headquarters in Connecticut and put in his company's bid for an opportunity to discuss the project with them.

A trip to their offices revealed that the firm didn't put their work out on bids, and that cost wasn't always the major factor. They were going to send a three-man team here, let them scout the territory, and find the firm that they thought would be best suited to do the job quickly.

When they found such a firm, they would sit down and talk costs, date of occupancy, etc. What Greg didn't know was that there was a 60-day, unflexible deadline for occupancy. The plant had to be up and ready to roll in the 60 days following letting of the contract, or the contractor would be heavily penalized on a daily basis.

The field narrowed to three firms, Greg's and two others. He met with the three men and pulled all the stops in an effort to get a commitment on the job. This contract could mean the making of his firm and a step up the ladder for him.

After four or five hours the company representatives told Greg that his firm was the leading contender, but that they were concerned over the deadline. Could it be met before the due date?

This was the one thing that had worried Greg throughout the meeting. He was a salesman, not a steel, concrete, or building expert. He didn't know whether they could get the steel, the concrete, and the hundreds of other things the job would call for on such short notice.

Also, who could predict the weather? Who could say it wouldn't rain the first 30 days?

He called in the construction foreman. This man *did* know about steel and concrete and how much allowance had to be made for weather. And *right there is where he made his mistake and almost lost the contract.*

He had already taken up more than half a day of these men's valuable time, and the conference with the construction superintendent took three more hours.

The construction boss knew his business, and could reasonably assure them that the job could be done within the deadline. But he did *not* have the authority to sign for the company.

One of the spokesmen for the aircraft firm finally saved the day for Greg.

"Look, we want your firm to do this job. Your financial statement looks good and your record with your clients is excellent. Why don't you get someone in here that can say 'yes' or 'no' so we can go back home with a contract, signed and sealed? We're getting tired."

In the senior partner's office Greg outlined the requirements and the construction superintendent offered his ideas as to whether the job could be done.

"Greg, have you worked out every detail on the contract? Are you sure everything is in order?"

"Yes, sir. Their attorney, Mr. Young, here, says that it is all we need at this point for a binding agreement on both sides."

"Good. Joe, can we build this plant, to these specs, have it ready one day before the due date, and *guarantee* our usual perfect, turn-key job?"

"The only thing that bothers me is the weather. The storm season is coming up, you know, and if it was to start raining. . ."

"Never mind that. Can we build this plant, *rain or no rain,* if we work around the clock seven days a week?"

"Now you're talking overtime. Extra shelters, and. . ."

"Can we build that plant?"

"We can build it."

Greg's boss turned to the three men from the aircraft plant.

"Gentlemen, we can, no, we *will,* build your plant. *No* corners cut, *no* sacrifice of materials or labor shortcuts. But there will be *no penalty clause.* I am a builder, and my partner is a builder.

"We need this job, and this community needs your plant. But we will not take the job with an 'if-you-fail' finger pointing at us. We will build your plant and hand you the keys by the due date or go broke trying. But we do not *intend* to fail, so there is no need for a failure clause."

The three men looked at each other, nodded, and the deal was closed.

It rained 25 of the contract days, and the building site became a quagmire. Steel was held up, concrete due at three in the afternoon arrived in the middle of the night. But the plant was up and ready for occupancy two days ahead of the deadline. The executives even found their parking places marked with their names when they arrived for the official opening.

This was a near-miss because Greg had gone to *the wrong authority* for the answer to the "Can we do it?" question.

The construction superintendent was in a position to say that they could or couldn't, but not to commit the company. Valuable time was lost and in losing that time Greg could have lost the contract.

He is sales manager of the firm now, with a staff of five men, and he tells his salesmen to get the man who can go when they reach their limit. Don't waste time in between.

Go to *The Horse's Mouth.*

The Example Tag

Another tag-team approach that has proven itself time and again is "The Example."

When the salesman finds himself in a no-close situation, and has exhausted the ammunition available to him, (remember, you *never* use it all, or you leave your tag partner out on a limb) he calls in another salesman.

Rather than the manager or T.O., he resorts to the assistance of another salesman to make the tag more effective, and believable. In The Example he tells the prospect that another salesman had the same problem a week or two before, and that that salesman was able to resolve the difficulty to the satisfaction of all concerned. By problem, of course, he means *objection*.

Sometimes you *will* have a salesman who has just experienced the same trouble and has found a solution. If this be the case, so much the better.

If not, the trick is to get a man who is a *good closer* first, and who can think on his feet second. Get a man who's well known in the company for the fast close, the field-the-ball-and-pitch-it-back type who can get the job done with a minimum of conversation. This is of prime importance because you have already used up considerable time, so there is little if any to be wasted in talk.

In The Example you employ a bit of subtle subterfuge which calls for cooperation and teamwork on the part of the salesman and his tag partner. It is best in this type close to select a man who operates much as you do; a man you know, with whom you can work well; one you can anticipate, as the close is going to require that you stay with the prospect while the tag is in. In The Example you'll serve as straight man to your partner, and he'll wrap up the close.

Again, don't leave the prospect if you can avoid it. Get your partner in there without giving the prospect a chance to strengthen his defenses.

Then, when he's there it should be handled like this:

"Jim, you remember that deal you had a couple of weeks ago where the fellow had some securities that he wanted to cash in to pay for the furniture that he was looking at? I remember that the piece of furniture was the only one of it's kind and color that we had.

"I know you delivered it to him, but how did you go about

getting the deal straight, what with the securities transaction taking, what was it, a month, before someone else got there first?"

Here, you've given your partner a hint about where you need help, telling him, without coming right out and saying so, that your prospect wants to wait for his cash to come, and that your play has been that this is the only one you have; that you're afraid he'll find it gone when he gets back.

"Yes, I remember that sale. Mr. Persons. Nice fellow. A bachelor. Had to have that shade of green for his apartment, as nothing else would match."

Casual. Not a dive right into your prospect's objection. Now he's going to make light of the objection. Make it seem as if both of you are silly to even consider it a reason to wait. But *gently*.

"No problem there. I can show you how to handle it in five minutes with no problem at all.

"Mr. Jones, you're cashing securities to pay for this purchase? (Here, of course, the partner could make a pitch, in some cases, for the prospect to keep his securities and to finance, killing two birds with one stone. Or he can let well enough alone and play it straight.)

"Yes. No financing for me. I've had these two companies for a year now, and they haven't made me a dime, so I'm going to dump them. I need this furniture (house, insurance) but I don't need another monthly payment."

"I know what you mean. Who needs payments, eh, Mr. Jones? Well, I can show you how to handle it so there won't be any delay. You can get this set you want before someone else gets it, and we'll close the sale, for all intents and purposes, right now."

Here's where the subterfuge comes in, which is of course not unethical or improper. It merely lets the prospect think that this man is doing something nobody else in the company can do, and that he would not consider doing it for everybody.

"Mr. Jones, we have a special arrangement we offer to people of your circumstances that we can't afford to offer to everyone."

Then he tells him about the open account, or the 30-day plan which only costs one percent to carry. Of course if the prospect balks at this he gently tells him that he hasn't finished.

"You see, Mr. Jones, the beauty part is that he told you this was the price, but I can deduct the one month carrying charge as cash from the selling price and you'll arrive back at the same figure for the furniture. As the saying goes, Mr. Jones, there's more than one way to paint a barn."

Your partner didn't *say* you couldn't have done the same thing. He let the prospect decide that that was what he said. He didn't *say* he was a bit higher in authority than the salesman, for he wasn't, but he let the prospect decide that he was.

The prospect saw that he was getting something every customer didn't get; and that he was getting it from a man who had done the same thing recently for another *preferred customer,* and it had worked out fine.

In The Example close, your partner often demotes or downgrades you, but you're the beneficiary. He can paint you as the new man, himself the old pro; he can hint that you aren't thinking too well today; he can act angry with you for bothering him when the solution was so obvious. He has many options.

From where you sit the thing to do is *cooperate.* Play it the way he approaches it. If he wants to call you stupid and you know he can get the close, then sit there and *look stupid.*

Above all, let *him* carry the ball. Don't offer comments unless he tips you that he wants a comment by leaving an opening that clearly calls for one from you. Take his lead and *follow him.*

I'm Here Because It's Best

Larry had been trying to sell a prospect on installing automatic temperature control, intercom and central vacuuming for several weeks.

He had overcome the standard objections as to cost and need, and was ready to make what he hoped was the last call; the sign-up call. He asked one of the T.O.'s to go with him because he was a new man and was still a bit unsure of himself.

When they arrived at the client's home, the wife met them at the door and invited them in. They found their prospect in the den, going over a stack of brochures. This was an easily-spotted danger signal to the T.O., so he listened and waited for his chance, knowing what was coming.

After Larry had gone over the figures again and had explained to the woman, showing her how the equipment would work, where the vacuum outlets would go, etc., the man dropped his bomb.

"Gentleman, I appreciate your coming here tonight, and I'm quite sure you have the best equipment and the best price, but I want to look at this Elite," tossing a folder at Larry, "before we go ahead."

Larry's face fell. He had been so *sure* of his sale right up to that moment.

Not so the T.O. He saw the folders and knew what was coming. The old bugaboo, "I want to look around." A shopper.

Larry looked at the T.O. and mouthed the word, "help"', but there was no need. His partner had already tagged and his mind was racing.

"Mr. Jones, I don't know whether you know what a T.O. is or not. It means Training Officer. I am training Larry to be a good, dependable salesman—one his customers can rely on.

"And he's doing a good job for our company. Oh, there are men who sell more, but there is *no* man on our sales force who will look out for his client better than this fellow does.

"Now, Mr. and Mrs. Jones, this is my point. I am not supposed to help Larry sell. He is supposed to get or lose the sale on his own. I'm here merely to observe his manner and his sales approach, not to help him pressure you into buying.

"But for your sake I must say one thing, and let me repeat, I do *not* as a rule get involved in a transaction between my salesmen and their prospect. However, in this case I feel that I must.

"Mr. and Mrs. Jones, I am a professional salesman and an honest businessman, as is Larry. I was with the Elite people for two years as a salesman. I left when I discovered that the equipment Larry is selling you (*selling*, not *showing)* is a better product, even though it *is* slightly higher than Elite as far as price is concerned.

"We impress on our sales personnel, and we mean it, the fact that we have the best that money can buy, and the best service a customer can get, whether he bought it yesterday or ten years ago.

"I hope you'll forgive my butting in, but I couldn't help myself. Now, we've taken up enough of your time. Larry, shall we go on and let these folks decide what they want to do? You can contact them tomorrow."

"Mr. Cousins, you sit right back down. I'm going to have to use that vacuum, and I'm going to be in this house all day, so I have a say in this."

To her husband, "Honey, I think I want *this* kind. I like the way it looks, and Mr. Cousins is a professional. He wouldn't be selling it if he hadn't found out it was better than that cheaper one."

You *know* they bought it.

This was an *example*, although somewhat in reverse. The T.O. used an example of his own experience as a salesman *not to knock the opposition*, but *to boost his own product*, and it had gotten the close over a *lower priced* product.

Don't Send That So-and-So

A standing joke around one of the automobile agencies for which I worked for a long time was the old woman who told one of our salesmen, "Don't send that so-and-so, Dane." Only she didn't say so-and-so.

She came to the dealership early one morning, and I treated her just as I try to treat all of my prospects; with courtesy and all the kindness I can muster. Whether I said something she took offense to, or whether she just didn't like my looks I can't say, but something had caused her to dislike me intensely.

I had worked with her all that morning and half the afternoon, without success. I should have known there was something wrong, because she had found the car she wanted, the price seemed to be right, and she could afford it.

Yet she wouldn't go ahead. She kept telling me that she wanted to wait a while. Try as I did, I couldn't get that close to save my life. She left.

Then, late that afternoon, a woman called and asked for a salesman. Not by name, just a salesman, and just so it wasn't "that so-and-so Dane."

The switch-board operator was tickled and couldn't wait to tell me what had happened. I told her to put another salesman on, and he talked to her to see what it was she wanted.

She told him to bring the car she had selected, the *very one* I had tried to sell her, to her house and to pick up a check. As simple as that.

He asked her whether she was the lady I had talked to earlier that day and she allowed that she was, but that she wasn't going to do business with me. He asked her the trouble, but she refused to say, simply stating that she would take the car at the price I had quoted her, but that she would buy elsewhere rather than deal with me.

I told him to tell her that he would be there in an hour with the car, and he hung up. After we had all had a good laugh over the curious reaction the woman had displayed to my efforts, we agreed that the deal would be mine and that I would give the other salesman $20 for the delivery and subsequent handling of the woman.

I would stay clear of her and make no effort to discover her trouble or to placate her. I knew the problem, and knew it was not my fault. I knew even better that there was nothing I could do to change her mind.

It was a *clash of personality*, pure and simple. Only in this case it was one-sided, where it often occurs on both sides. I had no feeling of antipathy for her to match her firmly-stated averseness to me.

My name, the cigarettes I smoked, the color of my suit; any one of these could have been the basis of her dislike. I was certain that she didn't have a legitimate reason for wanting to deal with someone else. I had done everything in my power to sell her and to treat her with respect and courtesy in the process.

Personality clash is the strange and unpredictable something that causes a person to take an immediate dislike, no matter how prejudiced or unfair, to another person. Fortunately I had seen it before, and knew how to handle it.

I don't like long hair, mustaches, the hippie type, or young people who call me "dad" or "man." But I try to recognize that they *are customers*, and that *their money spends* just as well as anyone else's.

I once worked with a fellow, as good a salesman as I've ever met, who had a thing about pipes. When he saw a prospect take out a pipe, he immediately became furious, no matter how well he had liked the man before. This fury cost him goodness only knows how many sales until he finally learned how to recognize it and to cope with it in the only way possible.

I've seen salesmen who clashed with just about every human foible and habit there is, and customers with the same trait. One customer told me that he would never deal with a salesman who wore dark glasses because he didn't trust them. Another told me that when a man chewed gum it was a sign of immaturity; several salesmen have told me the same thing about their prospects.

What to do when there is an obvious personality clash? Tag, it's the *only* solution. When the salesman feels antagonistic to a prospect for any reason, valid or not, he should tag immediately and *get out of the picture.* No man can sell at his best when he dislikes his prospect, and there is no reason for him to lose a possible sale when he can tag and retreat.

He's Too Young for Me

Mrs. Weldon was a sweet old soul, as nice a woman as it's ever been my pleasure to serve. But she was hipped on the younger generation. They didn't have any sense, they were flighty, and would never amount to anything.

Had I known that she was coming that morning I never would have let Cliff catch her. He was a good boy, and a natural salesman, but he was young.

He caught her as she came through the door and told me later that she jumped on everything he said, took offense to it, and wanted to argue about it.

Fortunately he came to me before too much damage was done and asked for help. He told me the situation; that he had tried his best to treat her with respect out of deference to her age, but that he couldn't seem to get to her.

"Cliff, I'm going to give you a demonstration of personality clash so that you can be watching for it in the future. This case is one-sided, her against you, but I have seen it occur where both people disliked each other on sight. I'm going to take you back in the office with her and use her dislike to try for the close. In other words I'm going to use this clash to *get you a sale.* Just remember, *anything I say* is to get you a sale, and it is *not your fault.* It is just the way she is."

Back in the office, with Cliff looking worried and dejected, I spoke to Mrs. Weldon.

"Good morning, Mrs. Weldon. It's good to see you."

I could actually see her settle down in her chair, more comfortable and reassured than she was when Cliff came in.

"Good morning. It certainly is good to see you. Not that I have anything against this young man, of course. I just. . ."

"Don't apologize, Mrs. Weldon. Cliff is young, and has a lot to learn. You simply felt out of place doing business with a younger person. And then you know me too. Right?

"Now, is this the car you want?" I took up the spec sheet and examined it.

"That is the car I want if it is the one *you* think I should have. I like the color, and it's automatic drive, so beyond that I'll trust your judgment. Oh, and the young man's too, of course."

Nothing to it once we gave her a chance to slip a tiny needle or two into the "young man." For some reason, resentment of his youth perhaps, she was determined to buy from an older person, and to show Cliff that she didn't trust him or want to have any dealings with him.

This even held true after that when she came in with a problem. If Cliff tried to help her she simply thanked him and came looking for me. Not because she liked me especially, but because I was closer to her own age.

The Accidental Tag

This is a method of accomplishing the tag without interrupting the chain of the close procedure. It is relatively simple to accomplish, and very quick and smooth, but cannot be used in every tag situation.

The accidental tag can only be used when it doesn't matter especially who you tag with. In many cases of the Personality Clash, The Example, and The Authority it can be applied, provided the person tagged is not or need not be a specific individual.

In this tag the salesman simply waits for the first one who wanders by and tags him, with no preliminary, and no set plan. It is then up to him to give the incoming man a breakdown on what's taking place and where and how he needs help.

One ingenious trick I saw in New York was a buzzer under the salesman's desk. He could press it with his knee making it buzz right there in his office as if he were being paged.

The phones in the offices were connected directly to the other offices, including the sales manager's, and each had a separate line so that the phone could be picked up and would buzz the office the caller wanted.

When the salesman picked up his phone he would, in effect, be making a call out rather than taking a call, and when the party he needed answered it was a simple thing to fake the call and then say, "By the way, while I have you on the line, could you step in here a minute. There's something I want you to show me," or, "I think you can straighten out the problem here, you having more authority than I do."

This was still an accidental tag in most cases, as all the men were expected to answer the phone whenever or wherever one rang, in case another salesman needed help.

You Sure Are Smart, Mr. Jones

Every salesman gets his share of know-it-alls and wise guys. They are an inescapable fact of a salesman's life.

It is not, however, an inescapable fact that they can't be sold; in fact their attitude is often *founded* on the premise that they can buy, and *they know they can.*

Whatever the reason for their belligerence, sometimes based on a fear that they'll be sold by a salesman a little sharper than they are, don't run and hide when you see one of them coming—*sell him!*

We've already discussed the ways to field a man's objections and toss them back as reasons to buy. You can handle the belligerent or abusive know-it-all in much the same manner, and still get the sale in the process.

It is accomplished by simply agreeing with him and repeating over and over how smart he is. So if you're going to do that, where does the tag come into the picture? The tag sets the groundwork; lulls him into a false sense of security until it's too late and he's signed and delivered.

In your qualifying you're going to see what you're up against in the initial conversation. *Don't* lose your temper or get disgusted and insult him. That's what he *wants* you to do.

When he tells you that your product, service, insurance, or what-have-you is inferior, too expensive, or not right for him, let him think *he's selling you on his opinion and his feelings.*

When he's had his say and begins to run out of steam, excuse yourself and tell him you'll be right back. If you can act a bit flustered and confused, so much the better. When I use this tag approach I usually tell the man, "You're probably right, sir. I haven't been at this selling game long, and I sure have a lot to learn.

"And you obviously know what you're talking about, yes sir. I can tell you weren't born this morning. Uh, Mr. Jones, excuse me a minute. I'll be right back." Then walk off. Don't tell him where you're going or why. He knows. At least he *thinks* he does.

"Boy, I really gave it to that guy. I'll show *him* who he's dealing with. New man, too. Guess he's gone to get the boss. Well, I'll eat him alive, too. They aren't kidding me. Bet a nickel if I stick with it I'll get the best deal there is. You have to be tough with these salesmen; let'em know you're no pushover."

See the pattern? His put-on bravado is going to make him the same pushover he's trying so hard *not* to be when you bring your tag partner back and introduce him.

Not as the boss. Not as the sales manager, unless he is. A salesman is just as good, because your prospect has *convinced himself* that he's rattled you so badly you're going to bring in reinforcements from higher up. Let him believe *just that* whether you have brought them in or even if the man you bring in is newer than you are.

Brief your tag on the way. Tell him you have a wise-guy, and he'll know how to handle him.

"Mr. Jones, I'm Bert Peterson. Ed here tells me you know the ropes when it comes to buying (tractors, mutual funds or aluminum siding).

"To tell you the truth, Mr. Jones, a lot of people think a person who knows his business would be harder to sell, but that isn't the case at all, is it?

"You and I, being familiar with the way it is, know that an intelligent person who knows what's going on can be sold easier than the guy who really doesn't know what he wants, or how to go about getting it.

"That is, of course, if you have a good product or service to sell. One thing they can't do is fool us, eh, Mr. Jones?

"Now, the way I see it, you need this. . .and if we put it on the. . .and set it up like this. . .don't you agree, Mr. Jones, or did you have a better suggestion?

"Now, don't hesitate to speak up. You obviously know as much about this thing—or more—than I do. Ed, while Mr. Jones and I go over this to be sure it's right for him, how about slip out and get some coffee. How about a cup of coffee, Mr. Jones?"

Here's how you'll know he's all yours: properly handled, this fellow will *fight* to pay for the coffee!

So don't let the wise-guy get the best of you. Humor him, flatter him, agree with him, and then spend the commission from the sale you got from him.

You'll also see, as I'm sure you have, that once the sale is made he is a different person. He, *just as you,* was acting the whole time.

These examples of the tag-team close approach are only five of many. You can, of course, develop and perfect your own, the point being that *a concise, detailed plan is a must.*

No matter what its origin or who conceived it, follow it to the letter once it has been proven, and watch the closes come faster and easier.

As a great writer of a previous time said in slightly different words, "The plan's the thing." (Shakespeare)

4

The Double-Team Close:
How the Closer Nails the Sale

Walk Them and Lose Them

Jerry came to us as sales manager, and the week before he was to arrive, the firm's vice president and general manager told me that he hoped he hadn't made a mistake.

Ours was a conservative, low-pressure sales agency, and the manager was beginning to fear that Jerry, a fast-talking wheeler-dealer, might not work out.

He was wrong. Jerry adapted himself to our method of sales approach, and soft-pedaled his dealings with the customers in an amazing personality switch he adopted only with them.

The rest of the time he was his natural, dynamic, always-thinking self, and within three months his company and his sales force were the beneficiaries.

Monday morning of his second week we found a legal pad on the receptionist's desk when we arrived for work. It was neatly columned, with headings for the customer's name, his address, what salesman he talked to, and his purpose in visiting the agency.

Jerry told us in the sales meeting that each salesman would list his visitors, with an explanation as to why they didn't talk to someone else before they left. Most of use were disgusted at this juvenile treatment.

If they came for information or they were already customers, fine, but if they were potential customers, then they were not to leave without talking to somebody besides the one salesman.

When the pad was practically ignored the first week Jerry told us at the following sales meeting that every salesman who "walked" a prospect without "double-exposure," as he put it, would be fined ten dollars for every one he walked.

From the time we left his office that Monday morning to the close of business Saturday at 1 p.m., we had sold as much as we had the previous *month.*

We learned a great deal in the two years Jerry was with us; the most important and valuable lesson being the importance of the double-team.

What Is It?

How does a double-team close compare with the tag-team close covered in the last chapter?

It is very much the same, with one major exception: the tag-team close is usually a spur-of-the-moment decision to seek help with a difficult close.

The double-team is a planned-in-advance closing method in which you *begin* the close with two salesmen, sometimes because you expect difficulty, sometimes because you are on unfamiliar ground, or simply because your company policy calls for a two-man close.

The end result of an effective double-team is the same as the well-executed tag; the customer, exposed to the concentrated efforts of two salesmen, succumbs faster and easier than he would with one—a perfect example of the old saw about two heads being better than one.

Camels, Please

I saw an excellent example of the double-team in action at, of all places, a drug store.

My sales manager and I were attending a seminar staged by the great inspirational writer and sales counsellor, Napoleon Hill.

When we left the auditorium and started walking back to the

hotel, Jackie discovered that he was almost out of cigarettes, so we went into a corner drug store.

Behind the tobacco counter was a middle-aged woman who asked whether she could help us. A young man stood at her elbow.

"Camel Filters, please."

The woman turned to the young man and said, "Camel Filters."

He produced a *carton* of Camel Filters and laid them on the counter.

"I only wanted. . .oh, well, never mind. Do you have some matches?"

"Matches," again over her shoulder to the boy.

"Sir, we have a special on this week. If you have a minute I'd like to show it to you." The woman stood to one side and the young fellow reached under the counter and produced the "special," a cigarette lighter with two jumbo-sized cans of fluid and a box of flints taped to the box.

"This is the Blanco lighter, sir, and guaranteed to last forever, with a year's supply of fluid and flint, all in one package."

"By the way, sir, the lighter is already filled and the flint is in, so all you have to do is take it out of the box," the woman said.

By the time we left the store Jackie had spend almost eight dollars. We laughed all the way back to our room at the way in which he had been double-teamed, wondering whether they owned the store or were simply on commission.

With cigarettes selling at about 35 cents a pack, he had spent more than twenty times that much.

This didn't just happen. These two people had a *planned*, grease-smooth *double-team* going for them that surely *boosted sales immeasurably*.

Unlike the tag-team approach (they probably seldom made a sale important enough to warrant the time expended in a tag), they had practiced until they had an effective double-team working from the time we walked in.

And unless I miss my guess, the customers before and after us got the same treatment. They obviously operated on the premise, which is a good one to remember, that you don't get the sale you don't ask for.

They simply added the rider that two can do a better job than one.

The fact that *you should double-team wherever possible* should be obvious at this point.

Who?

The next question might be, "Yes, but who do I double-team *with? Who* is the best man to team with and what makes him best?" The role and identity of your partner is very important, and deserves further attention if your double-teaming effort is to bear fruit.

There are some general do's and don't to follow in double-teaming that closely parallel tag-team closing rules.

Never team with a person whom *you dislike* or with whom you are not comfortable. A good rule of thumb here is the fellow you think of for a companion when you go for coffee or to lunch.

Never select a fellow, no matter how well you get along with him, in whom *you don't have confidence.* If he is not a good closer he can't help you.

Always be sure your partner knows what the situation is; that he knows all you *know about the prospect* so he can team effectively and not open his conversation with the wrong comment.

Always match your partner to the prospect. Don't take a hunter to double-team a prospect who's active in wildlife conservation or an officer in the SPCA.

Applying the four basic rules, you've seen that the double-team partner, like the tag partner, may vary, but that you can stick to *one partner* if necessary provided that *you are compatible* and that you *fill him in completely* prior to the contact.

Experience dictates that it is best to keep the double-team approach variable; that is, use the partner best suited to the prospect and the situation at the time.

You will find that two or three closing sessions with each of the four. types found in any sales organization will prepare any two of you to work together smoothly and effectively.

Salesman

In many cases the best person for the salesman to double-team is another salesman. Not only because he may be more readily available and free to assist with the close, but because he does it every day.

The sales manager has other duties, and may not be available to assist when needed. Also, he doesn't close, or attempt to sell every day like the active salesman does, so he might have a tendency to "lose his edge," whereas the active professional salesman doesn't.

When you tag another salesman, put the emphasis where it belongs. *Don't* harp on authority, because the other salesman doesn't usually have it. *Don't* harp on how much better he is at selling, because the prospect doesn't want a salesman with a high record of closes working him over.

Do emphasize the fact that Joe had a sales situation much like this the other day, and he got it squared away with a minimum of difficulty or lost time.

Do emphasize that Joe has been here a long time and is better informed than all of the salesmen and some of the higher-ups. Keep it general, and favor the prospect's chances to make a good buy.

Two-Prong Double-Team

Just as a football coach tells the tackle and the guard on one end of his line to work the same opposing tackle who's been getting into the backfield and smearing his quarterback, so do the two salesmen double-team the prospect, wearing him down with a two-pronged attack.

The best way to apply the two-prong close is to concentrate on *team-work*. The salesman may start, leading the prospect back over the troublesome ground to let the partner get the feel of the situation and the problem.

The closing partner should *never interrupt* the salesman or vice-versa, but should watch the other for a sign that he's ready to turn it over to him, and pick it up the minute the conversation lags.

This way the prospect doesn't get a chance to build his defenses back, for he is too busy listening to the barrage that's coming at him first from one side and then from the other.

Divide and Conquer

I remember two fellows who worked in high-priced real estate.

They rarely worked separately, usually went on house transactions together, and had a practically foolproof closing approach that was as simple as it was reliable.

Their double-teaming approach could be compared to the age-old military concept of "divide and conquer."

When they arrived at the house they'd show the couple the major details such as bedrooms, baths, etc. together, these being items they would be mutually interested in.

Having picked the husband and the wife as to their individual interests, they would have selected this house because it had attractions to appeal to each of them, *but separately.*

When the time was right, one would suddenly remember the den. Not at all coincidentally, the husband would be a professor or a writer who enjoyed his privacy or a well-stocked library.

While that member of the team was showing the husband the den, the other would show the lady the elaborately-planned laundry room with space for a comfortable chair and a television table for her to relax with while the clothes were washing or drying.

It might be the outdoor barbecue pit for the amateur chef or the swimming pool or tennis court for the outdoor sports enthusiast, but these two salesmen had discovered that "divide and conquer" also applied to home sales.

Once the husband and wife had seen the provisions for their own comfort and enjoyment, they were much easier to sell on price and payments.

The above is a perfect example of the extra benefit to be had from the double-team effort, especially when the two men had worked and practiced together to create a *smooth-working partnership.*

Double-Teaming with the Sales Manager

An excellent example of the double-team close was worked with devastating effect upon my wife and I a few years ago when I was in the sales business with my own firm.

As a matter of fact, it was my idea, so it was applied more to my wife than it was to me.

I was at the right age to be a good insurance prospect. I was still young, had a wife and four children, all of them under ten, and I was making very good money.

Jim called one day and told me that he wanted to see me that afternoon. I agreed, my need for more insurance having been in my mind intermittently for months.

He came by the office and presented a complete insurance plan for me which would cover all my needs for the ensuing twenty-odd years with respect to college for the children, adequate income for the family in the event of my death, and a good monthly retirement check for me someday.

I told Jim he didn't have to sell me; that Betty was the one who would fight the plan. She had a good job in civil service, and she, the children, and I were in perfect health; she just wouldn't agree to the additional financial burden of a large insurance payment. I knew, because every time I suggested it there was an argument, Betty taking the stand that I shouldn't have to shoulder the payments in the event she stopped working for some reason.

Jim suggested that he drop by the house that night and bring his agent with him, a fellow who he said was a very persuasive salesman and "can always sell the ladies."

The three of us tried for two hours to sell her, but she stuck to her guns. I reminded her that we were talking about my chances to retire someday, that we owed it to the youngsters; in short, the whole line of sensible, logical reasoning that should have made a statue reach for the pen. But not her. She just couldn't see the possibility of my dying or her having to stop working permanently.

When she excused herself to go in the kitchen to fix coffee, Jim's boss waited a few minutes and then motioned to me that he was going in to talk to her alone. I told him to go ahead.

He stayed for ten minutes, and when they came out, him carrying the coffee tray and Betty following with a plate of crackers, she said, "Les are you sure you want to take on this burden even if I have to stop working?"

I assured her that it was what I wanted for all of us, and she and the agent put their heads together for about ten minutes while Jim and I sat there with our eyebrows raised, wondering how he had done in such a short time what three of us had failed to do in two hours.

He told me the next day on the phone when he called to set up a physical.

"She seemed to me like she wasnt't comfortable with all three of us hitting her at once; like she couldn't, or wouldn't give it any real consideration until she had a chance to mull it over, in her own element, you might say.

"Her kitchen is her sanctuary, her office, so I figured that was the place to talk to her, right there in her own kitchen, where she did her most serious thinking, over dishes or while she cooked.

"Then, while I was helping her get the cups out and the coffee started I told her about a friend of mine, a man of about your age and circumstances, who had died in a wreck a month before. His wife had a bad back and had to stop working; in fact, she couldn't even lift their two-year old.

"I told her that I had visited the widow a few days after her husband's death to find her wondering what was going to happen to her and the children.

"It was a real thrill to lay a certified check for almost $150,000 on the coffee table. She knew then that nothing was going to happen. Nothing, that is, except that she and the children would be able to live very well off the income from his insurance, never touching the principal."

Having heard this, you might say this wasn't a double-team at all, and that he could have gotten the sale alone; but you would be wrong.

He got that sale *because Jim was there* to keep me out of the kitchen *while he talked to my wife alone.* If the other man hadn't been there I probably would have wandered into the kitchen too, and we would again have been putting too much pressure on my wife. No sale until, as he said, she got a chance to think about it *in her own familiar surroundings.*

The Professional Closer

Rather than depend on sporadic, hit-or-miss double-teaming, many sales organizations provide professional closers whose job is to team with the salesman for the close.

These men are usually on standby, their only duty being closing, although in some smaller companies they are simply salesmen who are paid extra to serve in the closing capacity.

Either way they are always men of *proven ability;* men who have demonstrated their knack for getting the difficult close, and the salesman is wise to avail himself of their assistance *whenever he feels it might help.*

The effective professional is *close-oriented.* He need not concern himself with quotas (except for overall totals), prospecting, maintaining sales records, or follow-up of prospects.

His sole job should be to work with the salesman for the close, with nothing occupying his time or his mind except the close, and the best and most effective methods of achieving it for his men.

Follow—Don't Lead

When you double-team with a closer, *follow him; don't try to lead him.*

Before you joined the prospect you should have prepared him as to what to expect by way of objections, what sort of prospect he will be facing, and a brief background on the prospect so that he will be able to apply his talents most effectively.

The closer who knows his business and knows his men will use the salesman to hammer his points home or to emphasize an example. He will know how to give you a lead to step in and strengthen his argument and then retreat. But you must be able to recognize the point, when to step in, and when to retreat and hand the conversation back to him.

He is the quarterback. When he throws you a pass, catch it, but toss the ball back to him as soon as possible. If you both try to direct the conversation your prospect will be pulled this way and that, and you'll never close him.

How to Ruin a Double-Team Effort

Suppose we have Dick, the closer, double-teaming with Ted, the salesman. They're trying to close Mr. Perkins on a tract of land for a factory. The land is in a relatively new industrial subdivision, and there are three or four plants already there.

"Mr. Perkins, the Allied Paper-Cup Company will be your neighbors. They've been in there for about six months and they're really happy they decided to locate . . . ."

Ted interrupts, "They sure are. We had a time for a while there, though. Couldn't get water in to them, and they had a contract to start on. Had to work day and night to get those stupid public works people to . . . ."

"Yes, sir. Allied will be a good neighbor, too. They're in a related field. You said you manufacture paper wiping cloths for industry, I believe? You two can probably swap many of your supplies and things. The supply manager at Allied is a great fellow too. He . . . ."

"He sure is. Why, when I was trying to close him we went to lunch four or five times and he never would let me pay for anything. We've gotten to be real good friends now. Went fishing last weekend and . . . ."

See the tack this conversation is taking? Ted is not only *causing* the *conversation* to drift, he's missing the boat completely. If he would be quiet and let Dick handle it, which is his reason for being there, Dick would have a much better chance of helping him get Perkins' name on a contract.

This way would be much better: "Mr. Perkins, the Allied Paper-Cup Company will be your neighbors, etc., etc. They're really happy that they settled on our place. In fact, one of their key men has become Ted's fishing partner, eh, Ted?"

"Sure has. Fellow named George Doe. Supply Manager. You and he could probably get together with supply shortages, you being in related businesses, and swap when you find it necessary. You'd like George, too."

"I'm sure he would. Now, Mr. Perkins, let Ted tell you about the spur the railroad is going to put in to our property right away."

"I talked to the railroad people today and they expect, etc., etc."

Here Dick throws the passes and Ted catches them and returns the conversation ball back to Dick *as soon as he's covered what Dick mentioned.*

The Everybody Double-Team

I worked in an automobile agency with a fellow who teamed literally *with everybody.* His customers, the girls in the office, the druggist on the corner, the beat cop, anybody. Here's how he did it:

When he had a prospect he combined the demonstration ride with an outside double-team. Sometimes he set it up in advance, and sometimes it was spur-of-the-moment.

When he took his prospect and the wife and children to the nearby drive-in hamburger stand for soft drinks, the curb girl would come up and say, "Hi, Mr. Collins. I sure love the car you sold me. And it's so good on gas. Believe me, that's important when you don't make any more money than I do. What will you have?" This did more good than two hours of sales pitch.

Of course the next time he went there for coffee he left a dollar tip, but that sort of help would be cheap at twice the price.

Sometimes he would set up a meeting with the body-shop foreman, and casually tell his prospect, "If you aren't in a hurry I want to see the body-shop man for a minute," the shop being at a separate location.

When the shop foreman came out he'd let him know that this was the prospect by saying, "Al, how you coming with Mr. Lowe's car? Is it about ready? I promised it to him at four, you know."

"Yeah, Collins, I know. And I know better than to hold you up. Boy, if I ever get to where I can afford one of those new cars you sell I'm gonna get it from *you*. You don't give a guy a chance to goof-off with *your* customers' cars. Yeah, I'll have it to you in a few minutes, okay, slave-driver?"

The druggist at the corner simply greets him as "my favorite salesman" and the cop on the beat says, "The used car you sold me for my daughter is doing fine, Mr. Collins. Sure appreciate it, too. We couldn't afford to get a bad one what with her in college and all. Not on my salary, anyway."

Double-teaming all the time. Not a long, drawn-out plan, but double-teaming all the same. Using *the efforts of another person* or other persons to *assist with the close*.

To sum up, *plan* the *double-team*. If it's going to be a meeting with you, your partner, and the prospect present, be sure your closer *has the facts*, knows the problems, and is briefed on the type of person he's going up against.

Let him lead the conversation and you follow, taking his lead and keeping it only as long as is *absolutely necessary*. That way he can execute his attack smoothly, and without unnecessary deviation from the target, the close.

Use the double-team at all times. Talk to the people in the shop if there is one, the office help, your other customers, or anyone who can give you a one or two line boost as you pass. You'll be surprised how effective it can be.

5

The Empathetic Narrative Close:
How a Story Can Put You
in the Big Leagues

Advertising Doesn't Necessarily Sell

The commercials you see on television with pretty girls in bikinis leaning against a Zoomer Eight, running their manicured fingers lovingly over the fenders, don't sell cars.

When the commercial shows two cars crashing together and the insurance company settling one driver's claims on the spot, while the other company's client waits months for a check, they are not selling insurance. They are *creating interest in their company* in the hope that someone watching is going to need insurance, or is going to be tempted to change companies, perhaps because of unsatisfactory service some time in the past.

The manufacturer's agents will tell you they *create interest*, help to get the viewer *thinking* about buying the Zoomer, but they don't *sell* the car.

It makes sense. If those ads *did* sell cars, then there would be no need for the expensive dealership with elaborate showroom and carefully-planned closing offices. The dealer would simply need a girl seated at a desk taking orders, and a service garage at the back of the building servicing and delivering the cars as the customers made their choices.

There are many other things the dealer could eliminate, including you, the salesman. He wouldn't need you with the commercials doing his selling for him.

So advertising does not eliminate, but rather creates a need for salesmen. When the viewer gets ready to buy insurance or change companies, some salesman gets a prospect.

Tell a Story

By the same token, however, when the salesman gets a prospect, he does *not* necessarily get a sale. In fact this is where salesmanship comes into play; this is where the salesman either earns a commission or loses the sale to a sharper, better-prepared competitor.

How did you get your job, your wife, that promotion you wanted so badly? You told a story; you *demonstrated* that you were the man for your boss or your wife; you *sold*, in this case, yourself.

Why does a horse-racing expert in need of animals for his stable follow the claiming races? Why do professional football teams watch replays of their opponents' games? Why do prospective buyers ask for proof of your claim that they should buy your product?

All of the answers are the same: the horseman needs to *know* before he buys; the team needs to *know* how to play against each opponent, and prospective buyers need to *know* that yours is the product for them.

Sometimes it's just a matter of telling the prospect that yours is the best. Some of them are trusting souls who will believe just about anything. They may simply like your looks or the color of the car you're showing them; the amount of the premiums, or the name of the insurance company you represent may be one of which they've heard; the house you show them may have a fireplace or an outdoor barbecue pit that strikes their fancy. *Sometimes.*

How many times has a prospect told you, "This wasn't the right one for me, but I let the salesman talk me into buying it"? Plenty.

And how many times have they said, "This is obviously the right one, and the price is right, but I guess I'd better think about it for a while"? Plenty.

How many prospects have you allowed to get away with this fright-motivated, put-it-off-as-long-as-possible delaying tactic only to contact them later and be told, "I bought one right after I left you"? You should have a dollar for every one, or, better still, you should have a *sale* for every one.

We all know these types are harder to close. These are the ones who require salesmanship; who require you to use that extra effort, that *extra clincher* to get the Big League close *now* before the competition gets to them.

These are the ones who *want* to go, who know they *should* go, but can't quite make up their minds to take the plunge. These are the ones for whom the story is designed. These are the ones who are *begging you* to *tell them the story* they want to hear. The ones who are just *waiting to be told;* helped in making that decision which is so all-important to both of you.

So what do you, the salesman, do? You pounce on his interest and you bring the television commercial down to a personal, "I'm talking to you," level. You *tell* him exactly, and in detail, what the television commercial only hinted at. You give him something that he can *identify* with, tell him about his neighbor's experience with your product; about the company in his area that is already using your trucks or the fellow down the street who wrote to tell you how happy he is with the insurance plan you sold him. *Help him identify,* help him see his *need* for your products *here and now.*

Tell him a story, and watch it put you in the Big League.

Facing the major decision to buy or not buy leaves a man standing alone; frightened, vulnerable, and wracked with indecision. Then you come along and offer help by relating stories of people who found themselves with the same decision to make, and tell him what they did to arrive at the right one.

Whether consciously or unconsciously, he will be glad for your help. He'll welcome a story that tells him how that person made the decision and he'll welcome proof that it was a good decision.

The story has to fit the situation. It may be the shocker; a simple talk on the product's merits, with examples of how some other firm or individual uses it; or it might take the form of a demonstration or trial of your product.

The Subtle Shocker

Carl called me late one afternoon and asked me to have a drink with him before I went home. He said he had a problem prospect with whom he wanted my help. I agreed to meet him and the prospect at a downtown oasis later that day. I told Carl not to mention a thing about selling the man insurance. He had prepared a complete folio on the fellow, a businessman, and was going for something like $87,000 in one order and nearly that much over the next few years. I told him to go to the appointed place and let me just "happen" to come by. When he saw me he was to invite me to their table, let me lead the conversation, and take his cues from me.

I have never sold insurance. I believe in it, I have a bundle of it, many of my friends sell it, but I never have. This I know, however: the insurance prospect is no different than anyone else who's considering a purchase. Told the right story at the right time, with the right emphasis and slanted to his needs and desires, he'll buy.

I arrived at the club and found Carl and his prospect chatting quietly over a drink. On the way to the meeting I planned my strategy to help Carl close the deal, preferably right there and then.

He had done his homework well and had consequently developed a good plan. The prospect was young, married, and had two children. He had a good job as an executive in a large, busy construction firm and his future seemed bright.

Equally important, he had contacted Carl's agency in answer to a questionnaire sent out by the home office, expressing an interest in more insurance.

He had shown the interest, the need was there, and the ability to buy was there; Carl simply hadn't been able to wrap him up. The prospect was caught between Carl's plan and one from a competitive agency, which I'm sure was equally as attractive as Carl's.

When I walked by, Carl grabbed my arm.

"Hi, Les. How are you? How's the family?"

We chatted for a minute or two, and Carl introduced his "friend."

"Why don't you join us, Les? We're just having a drink. Come on, pull up a chair."

"Well, I don't want to interrupt anything important. . . ."

"You aren't interrupting anything. Come on." The prospect

reached for a chair and drew it up for me. I could see his thoughts clearly:

"He won't dare try to talk insurance with his friend sitting here, so I'll have another day or two to make up my mind without offending him."

Indecision!

Carl had told me about a friend of ours, thirty-odd years old, who had dropped dead the day before. Fortunately he lived a hundred miles from us, so it was a good risk that the prospect—we'll call him Tom—didn't know our deceased friend had carried plenty of insurance.

"Carl, I guess you heard about Eddy's fatal heart attack the other day. I sure hated that. He was a nice guy. But, you never know when your time will come, eh, Tom?"

"That's right. 'You never know,' is right," Tom replied.

"Carl, if I remember correctly you sold him some insurance. Did he have enough, a plan or something, or was he like me. . .you had to shove him all the time to get him to carry enough to protect his family? Had two youngsters too, didn't he?"

Carl took the cue beautifully. As I watched Tom, his eyes downcast, staring into his drink, Carl said, "No, as a matter of fact, I feel I let him and his family down. Maybe I didn't push him enough. Maybe I should have. . ."

"Uh, Carl, about that plan you worked out for me. I'm not scared, mind you, but. . .would a check for five hundred now put it into effect so, well. . .you know," he was reaching for his checkbook, "I'm 43, and I've got three boys."

"Look, Tom, I didn't mean to scare you. I. . .". I prenteded surprise that he was a client of Carl's.

"Think nothing of it, I'm glad it happened. The next round, gentlemen," he grinned as he made out the check, "is on me." No more indecision.

The timing was right, and the story made sense. It was a case Carl's prospect could *identify with*; a situation that *could have been him,* and it brought a close in minutes that Carl had been after for weeks.

The Ice-Water Dip

The lady was a widow, and quite elderly. I was a T.O. at a large automobile agency, and the salesman, a new man, had run into a snag at the close.

The woman had an old car, with over 100,000 miles on it, but it still looked and ran like a new one. She couldn't make up her mind to trade her old car, parting with $3,000, as long as it performed as well as it did. She wasn't the least bit interested in trying to impress the neighbors, and said she could care less whether she had a new car.

When Al came in and told me he was having trouble with her, and that she had just about talked herself into keeping the old car, I used what I call the "Ice-Water Dip" going for the close.

I told him to bring her into my office, close the door, get her sitting down, and let me take it from there.

I had told Al not to tell her anything but that the sales manager wanted to meet her before she left. When they walked into the office I was standing by my desk with the *New York Times,* reading.

He introduced us, ushered her to a chair, and sat down. I walked slowly behind my desk, a worried frown on my face, still holding the paper.

I threw the paper on the desk and said, "Mrs. Carter, I don't know what this country's coming to. I was just reading in the *New York Times* about another mugging. They beat an old man half to death and left him lying on the freeway. I just don't know what we're. . . ."

"My goodness, did they kill him?" she interrupted me.

"No, fortunately they didn't. Seems his car broke down and they, four young fellows he said, stopped to help him, or at least he so thought until it was too late. Poor old guy, trusting those punks!

"But let's get to you, Mrs. Carter. Al tells me you selected a real nice car, and that you like the price. You have the money, so how is it we can't sell it to you?

"You know, we feel it's not only our job to *sell* the company's product, but also to *advise* and *take care* of our customers to the best of our ability.

"I tell the salesmen, especially in a case like yours, you being a widow with no one to look out for you, to offer all the help and advice they can. Your car has more than 100,000 miles on it, and. . ."

"Young man," she stood up and shook her finger at my salesman, "you have that new car ready for me at three o'clock. I'm not going to have any young ruffians beating *me* up because my car broke down. I'll be back then, and you be sure my new car is ready, and that it won't break down with me, you hear?"

She left, and Al had a sale he almost lost. He also had a good demonstration of the story changing the prospect's mind when she had decided to make the old car do for a while longer.

In both of these cases the closing story was radical, but both sets of conditions called for a radical close, either the "Ice-Water Dip" or "The Shocker".

In the second example there *was* a story in the New York paper about an old man in an old, broken-down car. And he had been beaten and robbed just as I told her.

But rather than get the "ice-water" too cold and scare her so badly that she might stop driving altogether, I didn't tell her that he had been assaulted on the freeway into *our city* only a few blocks from where she sat.

I chose instead to let her assume that it happened in New York, a thousand miles away. After all, the story *was* in the New York paper.

The story in this case was strong, but milder than the first, or the "Ice-Water Dip" story. It was softened considerably, and much of the shock effect taken out by our concern for her, without reducing the effectiveness of the closing aspect of the story.

My little speech about her helplessness impressed her. . .showed her we were *concerned* about her safety as well as interested in selling the car. She saw that we were *ready to look out for her* in the future.

The proof of this by-play was that she called Al every time she encountered a minor problem, and he sold three new cars and a late-model used one in the next two months, all to her friends and family.

Show and Tell

A few years ago a "new teaching innovation" was widely heralded throughout the country. This "new innovation" might have been new to teaching grammar school, but it was one of the oldest sales techniques in the world. The educators call it "Show and Tell," but you know what it really means: demonstration; demo, for short.

The teaching method is remarkably similar to the selling version. The teacher tells the students to bring something of interest to themselves to school, and tell the class about it.

It might be a plant the pupil grew, something he made, a pet, or any number of other objects of interest.

When that student stands before the class and tells about his pet alligator or the model plane that he built, he is *selling; closing* a *sale.* He is closing a sale of interest in his pet or plane to the other pupils.

If it's a model plane he will more than likely interest one or more of his classmates in building models. If it's a pet he has taught to do tricks he will probably interest some of them in teaching a pet, too.

He is selling; making a carefully-prepared sales presentation. And if he does his job properly, he is closing that sale just as if he were trying to *sell* that pet or model plane, rather than simply talking about it.

Demo over the Ocean

A friend of mine owns an aircraft agency. It isn't a large firm, as he has only the sales, parts, and service franchise for one state and part of an adjoining state; but it's a sound business, and well-run.

We were chatting one day at a civic club meeting when he told me that his repair and parts business was good, but that sales were off; in fact that they had never been what they should have been for an agency the size of his.

I was curious about this, so I asked him how he handled his sales business. How did he locate his prospects? Did he concentrate on business firms for his sales, or individuals and flying clubs? Did he employ a salesman, etc.

He told me there was one salesman who was also a pilot, and that they got prospects from the usual sources; referrals from the parent company, watching for badly damaged planes in the shop, and calling on business firms. He said but they depended primarily on sales to business rather than individuals or clubs, but that there simply weren't enough of them.

There was no clear reason for his sales to be off, so I offered to look his place over, meet his salesman, and try to put my finger on the trouble.

Seeing his place didn't help. It was neat, with attractive buildings, adequate service facilities, and a nice concrete strip of sufficient length to handle any aircraft he might need to accommodate. The receptionist was attractive and pleasant, and the salesman was a good-looking young fellow who seemed to be eager and well-informed about the airplane he was selling. I did get a clue, however, when he told me he had designed a plan to increase sales, but that his boss, Dino, had nixed it as being too expensive.

We went to his office for coffee and while we waited for Dino to get back from lunch, he outlined his plan. I decided that it wouldn't necessarily guarantee sales, but at an initial cost of $3,000 to put it into effect it could be a step in the right direction if a few figures Dino could supply were about what I estimated they would be.

We went out on the landing strip where he showed me his demo plane, a six-passenger executive job with all of the latest radio and navigational equipment. It also had a flying office, complete with typewriter, adding machine, copier, and the other miscellaneous gear for a good office.

The demonstrator was the key to his idea. As we talked, Dino came up and asked whether I had bought a plane yet.

"No, Dino, I haven't. But I think this young man has come up with the solution, or at least part of the solution anyway, to your sales slump. I'm not in the market to buy a plane, but if you'll listen for a few minutes I'll bet I can help you and Bob sell some."

"How?" He was suspicious right away, on his guard, knowing I was going to suggest he spend money he didn't think he could afford to spend.

"Let's go in your office. I need some figures and some facts from your files." I took him by the elbow and steered him into his office.

I asked for the files of his advertising budget for the previous year, the sales figures and gross totals, and his operating statement.

"Now, before you tell me Bob's plan is too expensive, let me see an invoice for one of those six-passenger jobs like Bob flies, a basic model, without all the extras, so I can figure how many we'll have to sell the first 30 days to justify you forking out three grand."

The plan was to contact buyers for four of the larger factories and industrial firms in the area and invite them to fly, at Dino's expense, to Nassau for a weekend, with no strings attached.

Dino produced the figures I'd asked for and I saw that one sale of the $20,000 executive would more than justify the trip. He told me he would go along, but that he was still skeptical, and that if we got one sale he would give us a bonus of $500 apiece.

I briefed Bob on what I wanted him to tell the buyers when he called them. He was to say that it would be "business as usual"; that they were to make no plans for being away from their offices—that we would show them it wasn't necessary.

We boarded the plane at Dino's plant after a tour of the shop, and flew south toward Florida and the Bahamas.

A few minutes after take-off the sales manager of a large chemical firm called our bluff, or at least thought he had.

"I forgot to dictate a letter to the home office. Guess I'll have to wait, but that letter is going to be late, and I'm going to get chewed out. It's pretty important."

"No need to wait or get chewed out, sir. Miss Whaley, would you take a letter, please?" He was about to find out, as Atlanta slid by beneath us, why the girl was aboard.

Before our guest boarded the plane Bob and I had covered and concealed all of the office equipment so that it was virtually impossible to tell there was anything of that kind aboard.

The letter finished and typed, Miss Whaley called Dino's office on the radio, dictated it to the radio operator, and told him to mail it at once, with an explanation that a signed, confirming letter would follow.

"Mr. Nielson, you could have dictated the letter straight to the operator, but I thought you'd want a copy for your files," she said.

Nielson shook his head in disbelief as Miss Whaley handed him his copy of the letter.

More letters, a call to an executive's wife to remind her to make a bank deposit, and a three-way conversation between one of our passengers, his lawyer in one city, and his branch office in another; all from 5,000 feet over the ocean.

And so it went for the entire flight. We got the men stock quotations, a local weather report and even the latest baseball scores; things that would be impossible on a commercial flight.

The weekend in Bermuda was a mixture of business and pleasure, and before it was time to take off for the flight back to the mainland, two of the executives were seriously considering taking flying lessons, and a third, the chemical company sales manager, told us he was going to request permission to buy a plane as soon as he got back.

I had another good thought on the return flight. To demonstrate that the modern plane is easy to fly, we let each of them take the controls, and with only a few minutes of instruction they all handled the aircraft like pros.

Several months later Dino called to tell me he was setting up the "Executive's Guest Flight," as he and Bob had dubbed it, to fly executives to Nassau, at his expense, once every month in an effort to promote business.

"Show" is often as important as *"Tell,"* especially in the larger sales fields such as land, industrial and military sales, and other single transactions involving large sums of money.

In cases of this nature the salesman often comes up against professional buyers, men who are just as well informed as buyers as the salesman is in his field. They know what they want, and they often take straight sales talks with a grain of salt; they want to *see* what they might buy, and want to *watch it perform.*

Advance Planning Pays Off

I recall another instance of "Show and Tell" netting a nice sale and a fat commission for an enterprising salesman who was willing to gamble some time and effort on a sales demonstration.

Nathan was fresh out of high school, and only eighteen, but he was a smart, level-headed lad who had demonstrated through two summer vacations that he was going to make a great salesman.

A young executive, general manager of his father's chain of eight dime stores in five cities, told Nathan one day that they had never been able to have a satisfactory sales meeting.

He explained that with that many stores in a 200-mile radius, a telephone hookup was too expensive and left room for misunderstood orders. He was looking for a method of setting up sales meetings with seven or eight of his executives at one time, at one location, without having to get them together in a motel.

"Every time we meet at a motel or hotel it costs the company two to three hundred dollars, and there's always the problem of trying to get letters typed, orders sent out. . .that sort of thing."

That got Nathan thinking. Why not a bus, set up with a shower, kitchen, office equipment, and telephone? It would be a mobile office and meeting place that could go to the key executives for meetings.

He wrote some letters, and in a week or two had the facts. For about $16,000 a house-trailer firm would equip a truck chassis with a complete traveling office, along with power steering, power brakes, and air-conditioning.

He took his brochures and letters to the dime-store executive and showed him the plans.

"Can I see one, Nathan? It sounds exactly right for us, but I'd like to see it before we go ahead."

Nathan had anticipated him. "There's one in a small town about twenty-five miles north of here. The man is a contractor from New York, and he's developing three large tracts of land near there. He travels between fifty and a hundred miles from one site to another, and takes his secretary and bookkeeper with him."

That weekend they went to see the mobile home-office and got a contract for one equipped the way the store executive wanted it and Nathan got a commission of more than $800.

This is one more excellent, proven example of what going to the extra trouble to demonstrate your product can do.

Tell him a story that could apply to him; that could have *been* him, and he'll grab the pen every time. By telling him a story you are helping him decide; you're justifying his decision to go ahead with your product, and this is just what he wants; to be helped with the decision; to get it over. Help work that Big League Close.

Show, Tell or Both

There are many variations of The Shocker, The Ice-Water Dip, and the demonstration, and no two salesmen will use them the same way.

Work out your own. Some men prefer to set them up ahead of time for each general type; the "I'll-check-back-with-you-later," the

Pro, or the one who can be closed with a simple sales talk. Some prefer to "fake it," that is, set it up as they go, with no real plan until they're ready to go for the close.

The way in which you do it is not important, just so long as you *do* it. Tell it in your own way, fitting the talk or the demo to the prospect as the situation develops, but remember: *Show* and *Tell,* or *Show,* or *Tell; TELL A STORY.*

6

All in Favor Nod Your Head:
Three Basic Musts and
Four Ways to Apply Them to the Close

Don't You Agree?

One of the most amazing examples of mass hypnosis I've ever seen was at a sales seminar in North Carolina. The man at the lectern was a graduate of several colleges, a very successful salesman and manager, and an authority on psychology as it applies to salesmanship.

He told us that sometime during the first day of the seminar, which was to last three days, he was going to "hypnotize" all of us from the front of the auditorium, and that we would be unable to tell when he did it, or to combat the hypnosis.

Of course he didn't mean hypnotize us to the extent that we would bark like dogs on command or anything like that, but that we would be hypnotized all the same.

Midway through the afternoon, following a few standard lectures that you hear at all sales meetings of this type, he switched tactics, barely, and very smoothly, but a switch all the same.

The change was more noticeable to some than it was to others, but it was nothing radical or startling, so most of us forgot about the mass hynotism. Until the third day, that is.

He had been telling us, *selling* us, on the importance of keeping the prospect thinking positively; of keeping him in the "buy" mood or the "yes" mood. This had been the theme of his talks for the entire two days-plus.

After lunch the third day he told us that they had set up a projector, and that the man with the movie camera who had said that he was taking pictures for the school's management, was actually part of his demonstration of mass hynosis.

He had, in his switch, lulled us with questions easily answered in the affirmative, and every now and then had inserted a ridiculous one.

As the camera panned around the room we saw ourselves, *nodding in agreement with every word he said*—the camera occasionally swinging to him, nodding his head up and down, up and down, as he talked, soothingly, smoothly.

We were so busy agreeing that some of us, me included, had gone right on nodding with him when he said, "If a customer refuses to sign, you should, as a last resort, slap his mouth, shouldn't you? Sure you should," or, "There are people living in this city who were born and raised on Mars. We both know there are, don't we? Of course we do." Nod, nod, nod, and us nodding right with him. . .hypnotized just as he said we'd be.

We were *not* half asleep. We were *not* drunk. We were *not*, in the true sense, hypnotized. We were merely responding to a carefully-prepared, well-executed, *positive thinking* sales approach that had us *agreeing* with anything and everything he said, and we had been *warned.*

You can tell the prospect how badly he needs your product or service; you can demonstrate the product until it's worn out; you can make concessions until your firm will lose money if you get the sale, but if his attitude is against the purchase, you'll *never* get the close.

The Cold Contact Is Not Cold

Essentially, the need to get your prospect, and to keep him, in a receptive, positive frame of mind, applies more to cold selling than it does to the prospect who has come to or contacted you in regard to the purchase.

Usually, what has been designated a "cold" approach is not cold, but "cool."

By cool I mean that when the salesman talks about a cold approach, he really means he didn't have an out-and-out request from the prospect or a firm interest shown in the product or service.

But he usually had *some reason* for selecting that particular prospect to call on, so the prospect is not cold, but cool. Even here he has a foot in the door, something to concentrate on when he makes his approach, and later when he goes for the close.

It is also true, however, that the preparation, the warming up of this prospect, may take more time and effort than the prospect who has indicated a firm interest in what the salesman has to offer.

The Three Basic Musts

Whether your prospect is "hot," or you're approaching a so-called "cold prospect," the sales talk always has three aspects that remain constant: you *control the conversation,* you *offer a choice* rather than a yes-or-no, and you *deliver your sales talk in a positive,* "nod your head" *nature.*

"Ladies and Gentlemen of the Jury. . . ."

Why control the conversation? Compare it with a jury trial.

The defense attorney is summing up. The law provides him with the privilege under the constitution of trying with every power he has, his voice, witnesses, or anything he can think of, to convince the jury, without interruption, of his client's innocence. For this reason the prosecution must remain quiet, the jury must listen, and the spectators must maintain silence. The attorney would be a fool indeed if he allowed the prosecution to argue while he was summing up. He would be lax in his responsibility to his client if he allowed the jury to question him, and he would not be an attorney if he permitted outside disturbances such as a noisy spectator interfere with his summation.

The prospect is the jury. The salesman must convince him that his argument, his sales approach, is true and factual, and that his product is the best for the prospect.

Of course the spectators could be likened to any outside disturbance or interruption that could break the chain of thought and progress toward the close, and the prosecutor could be the person who came with the prospect or some other opinionated bystander who should not be allowed to influence the prospect's decision.

These conditions and possibilities must be *controlled by the salesman.* Certainly he must answer or at least show polite consideration for his prospect's questions, but he need not allow, in fact, had *better* not allow, the prospect to lead the conversation, or he will never arrive at his goal, the close.

Yes and No

Why is a choice so important? Webster defines "no" as the "word used to deny, refuse or disagree; such as 'I will not,' implying a definite and irrevocable decision not to do this or that." Very *final* isn't it?

He defines "yes" as: "The word used to express agreement or consent, such as 'I will do this or that.' "

Doesn't sound nearly as definite and final, does it? And it *isn't.* You have found time and again that when the customer or prospect said "no" he meant exactly that and nothing else. Have you had a great many of these prospects come back, their minds changed, and say, "yes"? Not many.

These two words are direct opposites in more ways than one. When a prospect says "no," he *means* "no," and the salesman is going to have a difficult time trying to make him change his mind to an affirmative answer, if he can do it at all.

But when he says "yes," he more than likely means "maybe," or at the best, "yes, unless I change my mind, which is quite likely."

So we see here that the logical approach is to avoid the fateful word that closes the door to further negotiations, the sale lost, at least for the present. How?

Which One, Mr. Evans?

The simplest way to avoid the devastating negative is to *offer a choice.* You are controlling the conversation, so why not ask him which of two possibilities, or three, or four, he prefers, rather than asking whether or not he wants one of them. Which sounds better from the salesman's position?

"Mr. Evans, *can I* fix up the contract and bring it over?" or, "Mr. Evans, *when* would you like me to bring the contract over for your signature? I'm free this afternoon, or we could do it at your home tonight, whichever is more convenient for you."

In the first example the salesman has given him a clear shot to say "no," and he may have to do all his groundwork and selling over, if Evans will let him.

In the second he hasn't locked things up so tightly that Evans *can't* say "no," but he has made "no" a great deal more difficult; has offered a *choice*, rather than an ultimatum.

Does It Have a Starter?

The third requirement of a successful close approach is the "nod your head" vein of the talk, the *positive, controlled conversation*.

Which sales talk would be most likely to sell you if you went in a hardware store for a screwdriver and wandered over to "just look" at the power lawn mowers?

"Good morning, sir, may I help you?"

"Just looking, thank you. Came in to buy a screwdriver, actually."

"Oh. Uh, this is a nice little job here. Doesn't have a self-starter, but then you can't expect that for only $89.95, right?"

"Yeah, I guess you're right. Where are the screwdrivers?"

"They're in another department, sir. I'm not allowed to work over there. Commission, you know, ha-ha. Now this mower here has a...sir...sir? You're going the wrong way for the screwdriver department!" Leaves you cold, doesn't it?

How about this?

"Good morning, sir. Let me show you that machine. It's a real dandy, and we have a special price on it this week."

"Got a self-starter?"

"This one is designed for small lots of less than half-an-acre. Has plenty of power to get the job done on ordinary-sized lawns, and is the easiest thing in the world to start. It has this self-winding recoil, and of course the low horsepower makes it a baby's job to pull it over. The magneto makes for instant cranking, too."

"Well, I guess for my little lot it's big enough. Probably doesn't need a starter, at that. What's this knob here?"

"That's the choke, sir. Set it about half-open, pull the cord—it's unbreakable stainless cable encased in plastic—and watch it go to work. Go ahead, crank it up. It's all right."

"Runs good, doesn't it? Not too noisy either."

"Muffler. It's one of the first on the market with a muffler. How would you pay for it, sir, cash or charge? It's only $89.95 this week, no extra charge for the credit plan, and no down payment necessary if you should decide to charge it instead of paying cash."

"Well, I just came in for a screwdriver, but. . ."

"Yes, sir, you remind me about that before you go. And while we're at it let me show you the greatest thing you ever saw in grass catchers. It eliminates raking the lawn, catches the grass in this. . ."

Three guesses as to which salesman made the sale.

The Four Basic Approaches to the Close

Keeping the prospect's attitude favorable, leading the conversation the way you want it to go, and offering a choice rather than an ultimatum are fine, but these are *basic guidelines.* They don't *make the sale,* or show how to get the all-important close.

Talks with salesmen and managers have revealed *four* approaches that *will* lead to the sale, *will* carry the transaction to a faster close, and will, with your own variations, apply to any close you attempt.

The first, and probably most basic method is when the salesman, rather than concentrating on overcoming objections, places the emphasis on clauses or features of the service or product in which the prospect has shown an interest.

You noticed that the salesman selling the lawnmower jumped on the comment about the engine not being noisy. He could have elaborated on this with questions about the proximity of his neighbors and the prospects tendency to mow the grass in the early-morning.

The main thing was that he *stayed with the feature the prospect liked,* or was concerned about Rather than ignore the question about a self-starter, he answered it without letting on he heard it, or making a big thing of it.

He simply told the prospect, and then *showed* him, or rather let him show himself, that the machine started easily without a self-starter. Then he laid it on about the muffler when the man indicated that he might have a problem if the mower was too noisy. The result was a sale. You also noticed that he didn't *ask* for the sale. He didn't ask the man *whether or not* he wanted the machine, but rather, *how did he want to pay for it? He offered a choice.*

Then, to get it across to the prospect that he considered the sale made (positive thinking), he went on to the grass catcher. Of course he was trying to sell as much as he could, but the *primary object* was to get the man off the mower, assume that the sale was final, and get away from it by moving to a related product.

What If I Get Hurt?

This approach could be used the same way in the sale of insurance.

"Mr. Carter, Ed Gamble, with North-South Insurance Company. I understand you're interested in some life insurance?

"I'll just pull this chair over where you can see what I've worked up. Now this portfolio I've prepared covers you, as you can see, from now right on past the age at which you can expect to be retiring.

"Now, I'll need some questions answered to be sure we have the best plan set up for you."

Once he's covered the number of children, the retirement plan provided by the company, number of years to retirement, etc., he begins going over the plan.

"Now, for the present, Mr. Carter, I've added this 20-year pay. . ."

"How much is the premium?"

"At this point the premium is secondary, Mr. Carter, but we'll get back to it in a few minutes. Now this is the. . ."

"Suppose I get disabled. Who pays the premiums? My job isn't really dangerous, but we electronic techs get near some pretty healthy stuff sometimes. ."

"Right here, Mr. Carter. In the event of your disability *on the job or off,* the premiums are automatically paid for you, and the policy remains unchanged. Now, here's another benefit in case you get. . .etc., etc."

The salesman has found what his prospect wants. The things he likes, or is most concerned about. From here on he will *apply the pressure there,* and the close will come much easier than it would if he bucked his man, trying to overcome objections.

"The total premium, Mr. Carter, and this includes waiver of all premiums on all policies, is only $89.43 monthly for more than $ in life insurance, all of it the type that accumulates cash value and pays dividends. And if you were to become disabled, the premiums would be paid for you."

He told his prospect the amount of the premium, but the emphasis was on the *plus factors;* the *cash value* and *dividends,* the *waiver of premium,* and the *amount he was* getting for "only" $89.43.

How Do You Work This, Mr. Scott?

Another basic and effective approach to the positive attitude close is to let your prospect *tell you* what you're selling.

A salesman selling tractors to a farmer certainly knows how the attachments are connected to the draw-bar, or how he would go about setting the plows to cultivate cotton, but why not let the prospect show him?

"Mr. Scott, this is the J-196, four cylinder diesel that you asked for. It comes with hydraulic draw-bar and three-point hookup, but frankly it just came in, and the attachments are so new that I haven't had the time to figure out how they hook up.

"Let's see, now, I guess this goes on the. . .no, that's not right. . .guess I'll have to get the mechanic to show us..."

"Let me see it a minute. Never saw a tractor rig I couldn't figure sooner or later.

"Hey, this new swivel seat ıs nice. You know, young fella, I've been wondering for thirty years why they didn't fix the seat so a man could look back at his plows easier.

"Easier to get off, too, and that's important at my age."

There's *the key:* the farmer is proud of his knowledge of farm machinery, and wants to be shown that this is the safest, most comfortable and convenient model for him. A few provocative questions and he'll have this farmer selling the tractor to himself. All he has to do is ask what this and that does, point out the cushioned, weather-proof seat, the headlights for night work ("You're not so old and decrepit that you won't be doing some night work, I'll bet"), and the sale is as easy as writing the purchase order.

"Mr. Elrod, I'm Dumb. . ."

The other day I was to have lunch with a friend who sells one of the best mutual funds portfolios I've ever seen. When I got to his office, his secretary told me that he was with a client, but that he would be with me in a few minutes.

When he ushered his man out and they shook hands, both of them were smiling, so I knew he had wrapped one up, or at least nearly so.

On the way down in the elevator and while we waited to be served he told me about his prospect.

"This was the hardest close I ever got until I used the 'what does this mean?' approach on him.

"You know, the one where you act as though there's a clause in there you don't quite understand, and then tell the client that you think you'd better get help before you steer him wrong.

"I had figured this fellow for a smart cookie who would delight in showing me where I was too dumb to see what was perfectly plain and clear, and it worked.

"It was in the graduated investment scale as recommended by our planning department, and I understood it as well as the people. who set it up, but I didn't let him know that.

"I had to laugh. He started out saying, 'you take the first seven months, and you invest eighteen dollars monthly, after the initial investment of three thousand dollars, and for the second period of the same length of time you. . .' and before it was over he was saying, 'and then in the third year I'll still only be investing a few dollars a month in addition to the original money, because the returns from my first investments will be helping to carry me along.' It was beautiful the way *he sold himself* on the thing.

"There I was, the salesman, asking him questions about the plan, our positions completely reversed. I almost bought the plan from him," he laughed.

Funny? Yes, but deadly serious too, when you think about the check for three thousand that Gary had collected, and the commissions that would come his way over the years.

For a Few More Dollars You Can...

The demonstration can do more to help you get the close, especially with the hard-to-close prospect, then all the sales talks and tricks you can muster.

The reason is simple. Would you buy a four-thousand-dollar car, a thirty-thousand-dollar home, or a $90 per month insurance portfolio before you had seen what you're getting for your money?

No, you wouldn't, and neither would most of your customers.

I have sold a few things, a car here and there or a small parcel, without the customer shaking it down carefully and thoroughly, but only because that customer knew me, or was not as careful as he should have been.

So for the most part, use the demonstration, but *hold it in reserve;* keep it as a clincher to help if and when your prospect balks at the proposition you offer.

Of couse it is impossible to actually demonstrate an insurance policy or a mutual funds folio, but it is possible to "demonstrate" by telling or showing your prospect what another customer received and how happy he is with his purchase.

In many cases, it is possible to introduce the new prospect to the one who's already sold, which is also, in essence, a demonstration.

Over the Hurdle with a Demo

My father-in-law has a plantation of about two hundred acres under cultivation. I was visiting him one weekend when he was expecting a salesman to bring out a pair of tractors which he was thinking of buying.

A car drove up, and a fellow got out and asked for my

father-in-law by name. He introduced himself as the firm's salesman, and told us that the truck with the tractor was on the way.

I was surprised to see that he was wearing khakis, heavy brown boots and a leather jacket, quite unlike any salesman I had ever seen.

When the truck with the tractor arrived, he hopped up, pulled the ramp down, and drove the machine to the ground. He left it idling and joined my father-in-law, walking around it checking the tire size, the draw-bar hookup, and the fuel capacity.

"Joe, take it down in the field and get the plows hooked up while Mr. Bentz and I are talking, will you? And be sure the oil and fuel are o.k. I'll probably be leaving it, eh, Mr. Bentz?"

"I was going to drive it some to see how it handles. . ."

"Plenty of time for that, sir. I want you to see some specs first though, so you'll be able to appreciate what you're getting." (Positive thinking again!)

"Son, if you've seen one tractor, you've seen them all. I don't pay any attention to all those figures."

"Mr. Bentz," he was leading us back toward the house, "what does it cost you to run a tractor, for, say, a week? I mean plowing six days, for whatever number of hours you run it?"

"Well, gas costs me about $40 to $50 a week on each tractor, I guess, but I'd have to check to be sure. Why?"

"Two of these tractors will run all week on half of that in dollars and cents, and do twice the work in acres in the process. For example, if you're using a six-disc cutter now, with each of these machines you can use twelve."

"Young man, don't tell me those tractors will do all that. . . why, that's ridiculous."

I knew what he was up to. He had brought diesels, exactly what my father-in-law should have had five years before, and he could now afford the initial expense. I decided to try to help, and see what the salesman's reaction would be.

"They're diesels. And as I've told you, you should have had them years ago. Let this young fellow show you what I've been telling you for years."

"Look, Les, you stick to your business and I'll do the farming. I don't need anyone to tell me what kind of tractors I need."

The young fellow saw that he resented my trying to tell him how to farm, and shook his head, one salesman to another, to let me know he knew what he was doing and could handle the situation.

"Mr. Bentz, do you lose any gas out here? Any of your people have cars? They might, uh, help themselves, like they do everywhere else."

They sure do. Steal me blind, and that's for sure. I wish I knew how to catch them. . ."

"Just don't tell them about the diesels. One tankful of that and you'll not only find out who was stealing your gas, but you can stop trying to catch them. I'll guarantee their cars won't go ten feet on number two diesel fuel, and it's 18 cents a gallon delivered to your tanks."

"Yeah, and that calls for special tanks to. . ."

"We put the tanks in, sir, and maintain them. Keep the water out, keep them painted and clean, all at no cost to you. And we will buy your gas tanks and whatever gas you have on hand at whatever you paid for it."

This boy was a salesman. And the beauty part was that he still had the *demonstration in reserve.*

After my father-in-law had gotten up behind those twelve discs and snaked them through new ground in high gear with the governor holding the engine just above an idle, he came back beaming.

Less than an hour after he had arrived, the tractor deal was closed, and the salesman had a healthy deposit check until Mr. Bentz could get to his broker the following Monday.

I Bought One and I Like It

There is a variation of the demonstration that can be applied to the prospect who doesn't even believe what he sees, feels or tastes.

He is the fellow whose fear or distrust of a salesman is so deep that he can't reconcile what he has seen, can't bring himself to trust his own eyes. And believe me, this is a *real fear,* a real distrust.

This fellow needs to be exposed to an outside influence, like someone who has bought the product or service you're selling, and is satisfied. Your prospect will usually listen to someone like himself, someone with nothing to gain from telling him whether or not he's satisfied.

Once when I was T.O. at an automobile agency, I helped one of our salesmen sell a difficult prospect a three-seat station wagon, getting an extra boost from the prospect's wife.

The prospect was a family man with a wife and five children. He said he realized that he needed a wagon, but had been told that after a few months it would begin to rattle and *that* was the one thing he couldn't stand. In addition, he was understandably concerned about the fact that our wagon was $1,000 higher than the foreign job he was also considering.

Ed brought the man and his wife to me, along with the five youngsters, and explained the problem. We were showing a medium-priced American make, and the prospect was considering a foreign make of the "bus" style because he had heard they were "rattle-proof" and cheaper.

I went back over the disadvantages, that is, what I considered to be disadvantages of the foreign model; the rougher ride, the possible parts problem, etc., but nothing would move them. They were determined that a three-seat, conventional wagon would be too noisy and too expensive for their needs, although Ed and I believed different.

It was Friday evening, so I excused myself for a moment and called a customer of mine to whom I had sold a three-seater six or seven months before. He had seven children, four of them under ten.

"Mr. Cutts, when was the last time you and your wife had a steak supper on me?"

"Mr. Dane, you sure know how to open a conversation. What's on your mind? And be sure you remember the steak!"

"How do you like your station wagon, Mr. Cutts? You *and* your wife?"

"I told you last month when we came in for a checkup that it was the smartest buy we ever made. Why?"

"I have a couple here who are doing just what you and your wife did. They're thinking about a three-seater or a foreign, bus type, and I can't seem to convince them."

"Biggest mistake they'll ever make. Tell them I said so. My wife would tell them the same thing, too. You tell those folks. . ."

"*You* tell them."

"Huh?"

I explained that I wanted him to "happen to drop by" the place as soon as he could get there, and to bring the children so my prospect could see that he and his family were happy with the three-seater and not sorry that they didn't buy the foreign make.

I told him how to do it; to come to my office and interrupt us with some excuse or other and that I would handle it from there.

It worked beautifully. The two women got together, the men chatted, and before you could snap your fingers they were riding off in the Cutts' station wagon, Cutts bragging a mile a minute about the advantages of his over the foreign type, and Ed and I trying to ride herd on the ten children—Cutts' oldest was out on a date—and keep them satisfied until their parents got back.

In about ten minutes they were back. As they got out the prospect's wife said, "The only thing that worries me is that we've always heard that they rattle when they get some age. And believe me, if we paid that much for a wagon, it would get some *age* before *we* could afford to trade it."

Mrs. Cutts made the sale for us right then when she said, "Honey, if you're anything like us, with a car full of children you won't hear it if it *does* rattle, so why not have the extra comfort of the kind you want?"

The *outside influence* did the job. Of course we put the Cutts up to it, but they were *telling the truth* as they saw it, and they were *sincerely trying to help* the other couple.

We hadn't bargained for one development, though. Cutts made us treat the whole family, including the oldest boy's date.

The case of my father-in-law was a good example of the demo held in reserve and clinching the close when the prospect began to balk because of reluctance to change an old habit, even if for the better.

The station wagon sale represents the clear-cut benefits to be derived from using an outside influence to close the sale, or assist with the close, when the customer balks or considers another product or service.

To summarize this chapter, I'd say that you must *focus the conversation;* you must lead it in the direction you want it to follow, removing bricks from the overcoat as you go, and *always in control.*

While you're controlling the conversation, keeping it on the track that leads straight to the close, you must also rob your prospect of every opportunity to say "no."

By the same token, you must provide an alternative, a choice, or else you will defeat the very purpose of keeping him from the negative reply. Preventing his saying "no" is a part of controlling and directing the discussion toward the close.

The third basic rule which must be followed to *guarantee a smooth approach* to the closing situation is also a part of the controlling procedure: you must, if your prospect seems to be in a receptive mood, keep him that way, being very careful not to alienate him or cause a mood-change that will most certainly make your close more difficult if not downright impossible.

We have discussed several methods of accomplishing the three basic musts necessary to a successful close approach, each related to the other, and certainly you already have or can devise more.

Size him up at the start; determine his attitude, lead him according to that attitude, offer him choices rather than yes or no, and as the bricks are removed from the overcoat of sales resistance they will stay removed; the Big League close will be smoother, easier, and more frequently successful.

7

A Close Is Not Always a Close:

Six Big League Ways to

Guard Against Prospect Blackout

When Is a Close Not a Close?

A close is not a close if the prospect calls back two hours later, or the next day, to tell the salesman to hold up; that he has decided that he might wait a while, or that the product might not be the right one for him after all.

We all know it happens. It happens all too often, and it can safely be said that in most cases it was the *salesman's fault;* that had he done a thorough job at the close, wrapped everything up and delivered where possible, there probably would have been no attempted backout.

The well-prepared salesman, even when there is an attempted backout, will be equipped to handle it without having to go over the entire close again; without expending double labor or double time making the close stick.

Whether you're selling cemetery lots, automobiles, or mutual funds, there are two basic safeguards that are an integral part of every closing procedure. These two *backout safeguards* will prevent more prospect mind-changing or attempted backout than any words you can say or any action you can take when a backout occurs.

Sign and Seal (and Deliver)

The first of the two safeguards might very well be the most important, as it comes first in the orderly chain of events following the prospect's decision to buy.

This is true for two reasons; it comes right after the prospect's signing of the contract, and it applies to *any close.* The other safeguard might not be necessary, or even possible.

Once the prospect has inked the contract, or said he will take the product or service you've offered, *complete the paper work. . .all of it.*

Time and time again I've seen salesmen make the mistake of thinking that because Mr. Jones signed the contract or said that he would buy, that the paper work could wait.

Then an hour after the salesman left and went back to his office (I've had the message waiting for me when I got back), the buyer has had second thoughts, and called to say, "Hold up on the deal. I want to think about it," or, "I'll get in touch with you later."

Usually, the salesman will say, "What does he mean by that? He signed a contract and I'll. . ."

You'll what? You'll *nothing,* and *you know it.* If he decides to back out there is usually little you can do. Technically, a contract is a contract, but we all know that until a deal is *wrapped up* and the goods *delivered* and *paid for* the contract is really binding *only on the seller,* not the buyer. How many times have you seen the selling firm go to court or even make an issue of the fact that the prospect signed the contract and is backing out? Unless it might be a half-hearted appeal to the signer's integrity, very few.

The solution is to *be prepared* to wrap up the deal, *completely,* with *no tag ends* hanging at the close. Then you have a much better chance that the agreement will stick than if you have six more things to do at the office that day or the next.

The Traveling Office

Several years ago I was on vacation 1200 miles from home when we stopped at a roadside restaurant for breakfast. We were about 400 miles due north of the border in Canada, so I was quite surprised to have someone grip my shoulder and say, "Can't you stay on the job, Les?"

It was a fellow from my home town, a sales manager for a local boat manufacturing plant, who was making a sales swing through Canada, the Thousand Islands, and back down the east coast to the southern city where we live.

When I had introduced the family to Bert and he sat down to have coffee with us, he explained that sales had been off the past few months, and that he was trying to get them back up where they belonged.

"We've been making this swing, which was my idea when I went with the firm as a salesman, for five years, and lately the sales have started falling through. The man we use on this run comes back with plenty of orders, but then the cancellations start coming in.

"I analyzed the situation, and when you finish your breakfast I'll show you where the trouble was and how we've all but stopped the cancellations."

I knew something about his company; knew they were small by comparison with other manufacturers, but that they had a good product and an excellent service policy. They were also the distributor for two leading outboard motors and several inboard engines.

I knew that they made this swing twice a year, delivering the boats sold on the previous trip and taking new orders as they went.

Outside, he told me how his salesman had been handling the sales. He would simply take the order, get it signed, get a deposit check and then tell the buyer he would forward the papers and that he, the buyer, would have them in a "week of two."

"That week or two was *killing* us. Actually, we were telling the buyer that he had a week or two to *back out,* and there was no way in the world to stop him if he chose to do just that."

Outside, he walked me to a short-coupled tractor-truck. Hitched to it was a trailer loaded five tiers high, three wide, and four long. He had 60 boats on that trailer, at what I estimated to be about $1500 per boat.

At the back was a plywood box with a hinged door, which he unlocked and let down, revealing a complete office. There was a typewriter, pigeon holes with order blanks, contracts, receipts, and a list of the serial numbers of every boat and motor that the firm had in stock.

"I call in every night, place my orders and bring my stock list up to date. That way, when I get an order I can assign *the specific boat* to the prospect, not simply write, 'one red with white trim, 14-foot fisherman.'

"The object here is for the prospect to see that he has bought *that* boat, that it is *already built,* and that it has been *assigned to him.*

"Then I complete the *entire transaction,* except for the actual delivery. I wish that was possible, too. I'm never satisfied with a sale until it's signed, sealed, and delivered, but signed and sealed is certainly a step in the right direction.

"I sold 184 boats on my last trip and only lost four by cancellation, and that was a dealer up on a lake in Maine who was wiped out by fire two days after I saw him. In his case, I had completed the *entire deal,* and we might have been able to hold him to it had the boss chosen to. These simple changes, completing the sale on the spot, have worked wonders for us."

Sometimes the prospect is in a hurry or doesn't want to bother to take time with the paper work and all the signing until later, but this can lead to trouble.

Often when he says he's in a hurry or has another appointment the old *second thoughts* have already started and he's getting ready to try a backout.

Be prepared, as much as possible, with the papers filled out in advance to whatever extent they can be, the exact specifications of your prospect's purchase, and anything else that can be covered now, so you can *complete the sale* then and there.

If he is going to pay cash, why get a deposit? Go ahead and get the full amount. If he doesn't have a check with him, get him one, and if you have any doubts at all, take it to the bank and cash it before he has a chance to stop payment. You can come up with a dozen explanations for this later if you need to. A simple thing like that can discourage the backout attempt when he calls the bank and learns that you have cashed his check. It will, if nothing else, remind him that he *made a deal,* and that you acted in good faith, never dreaming that he might try to renege.

The Dummy Delivery

Bert mentioned the second safeguard. It is not always possible, but where it is, *deliver* as soon as you can.

Of course there are times, as was the case with Bert, when you can't deliver on the spot, but when you can, add this safeguard to the first one, and *deliver.*

In the case of an insurance policy that has to clear the home office, an automobile that has to be ordered or a mutual funds portfolio that has to be made up, you can't deliver, but with many products and services you can. And you can often make a "dummy delivery" when you can't make the real one.

I used the dummy delivery when I was selling cars. I had a demonstrator, as did all of the salesmen, so when I made a sale that I couldn't deliver, I put the buyer (he's really still a prospect) in my car.

If he objected, saying that he didn't want to deprive me of my transportation, or that he didn't want to be obligated for the demo car, I insisted even more. I insisted because I felt that this was more often than not the *beginning of second thoughts* about his decision to buy. I knew that if I got him in my demo I'd be closer to eliminating that second-thought backout. In fact, I knew that by *obligating* him to me and my company, the very thing he was afraid of, I stood a better chance of keeping him sold. And he knew it, too.

I'll Go with You

Another trick which one an insurance salesman showed me is very effective in advance combating of the second-thought bugaboo. He did all of the paper work he could, got the necessary signatures and wrapped up everything he could.

Then, when he scheduled the medical check he told the prospect, once the appointment time had been decided upon, that he would pick him up, say, 30 minutes beforehand.

"I can find the doctor's office. There's no need for you. . . ."

"It's all right, Mr. Jones. It's part of my job, and besides, I have to see the doc myself for a minute or two, so I'll kill two birds with one stone."

Then he moved right on to something else or got away from the buyer if he was finished, so he couldn't insist that he not pick him up and deliver him for the physical.

He accomplished three things by handling it in that way: he headed off a possible change of mind later on, and he *spotted the potential backout* if there was one developing. And, if it *was* developing, he was in a better position to combat it, having prior warning. He also *further obligated the buyer.*

Having all the paper work finished and contracts and agreements signed is a *psychological deterrent to prospect backout.*

Going a step further, where it is possible to deliver at the close, it is extremely rare that the buyer will try to renege, and if he does the salesman has a strong lever, the delivery, with which to force the buyer to honor the agreement. Few prospects would go to court and admit they took delivery on a product or signed a completely executed agreement and then decided to back out of the deal.

One successful salesman told me, "Delivery of the purchase is the point at which I begin to figure my commission. It is not only rare that the prospect will attempt a backout once delivery has been made, but this is also the point at which I can, if necessary, exert pressure to force him to honor his commitment. Once he accepts delivery the deal is closed as far as I'm concerned, and there is no backing out."

Do everything you can to wrap up the sale, including the delivery wherever possible, and if you can't deliver, use these other tricks to obligate your buyer to stick to the deal he made. The harder you make it for him to renege, the more sales will wind up in your "Closed" file.

Back-In

When you haven't made the delivery, haven't gotten all of the money, or haven't had an opportunity to wrap up the paper work for one reason or another, you need at least one of the three "back-in" methods.

Back-in methods are exactly that. They counteract the attempted backout, and bring the prospect back in to honor the deal he made.

Essentially, this can be accomplished in one of three ways: *persuade* him to do what he agreed to do, make him go ahead out of *sympathy* for you, or *force* him to honor the agreement he signed. There are many ways to combat the actual backout attempt, and you can develop your own versions of the basic methods.

Guilty Conscience (You're Kidding!)

One of the most successful salesmen I know explained his favorite "back-in" method.

The prospect trying to renege on a deal feels guilty about it. He knows that he's doing the salesman wrong, that he made a deal, and that he should honor that deal.

Knowing that he has that guilty feeling I use his conscience to make him go ahead, the method depending upon the individual prospect.

Let me give you an example of what I mean, with a fictitious, attempted backout conversation on the telephone.

"Mr. Harris? This is Jones. You know, I was in there a couple of hours ago and looked at a Zoomer Deluxe."

"Yes, sir, Mr. Harris. You *bought* (just the tiniest emphasis on "bought") the blue four-door."

"Uh, yes. Well, Mr. Harris, I've decided. . .I mean, you understand, I like the car, and all, but. . .well, I've decided to wait a while before I buy."

(Here I wait a good 30 seconds before answering; to show that I'm incredulous; shocked that he could even *suggest* such a thing; letting his *conscience* work on him.)

"You want to. . .wait?"

"Yes, sir, I hate to do you this way, but. . ."

"Ha, ha, ha! Mr. Jones, that was a good one. You had me going for a minute, there. For a minute I actually thought you *meant* it, that you would really *back out on the agreement you made,* (notice that emphasis again), but I see now that you were kidding me."

"But, Mr. Harris, I. . ."

"Ha, ha, you know, it's a good thing you *are* kidding, Mr. Jones. (The 'But Mr. Harris' has shown he means it, so I go a bit stronger.) All of the papers are completed and the man is on the way to the highway department to register the car in your name. Should be back in a few minutes, in fact. Now, what did you *really* call for, Mr. Jones?"

"Call for? Oh, yes, I, uh,. . .I just wondered what time I can pick it up. You told me, but, uh, I. . .forgot."

"Sure, Mr. Jones. I'll have it ready. . ."

This fellow was just *feeling me out* when he called, wanting to get my reaction to the attempted backout before he pressed me.

In fact, you could tell by his voice and the way he stammered that he was really halfway hoping that I would refuse to let him renege, or that I would talk him out of it.

He explained his approach to the man who apparently has set his head, and is definitely going to back out of the deal.

"Mr. Harris? This is Jones. I was in a while ago and looked at the Zoomer Deluxe. Hold the paper I signed and I'll get in touch with you. Something has come up that means I'll have to wait a while, but when I buy I'll be sure to see you..." (Notice the reference to the papers. Every person attempting a backout will be *uneasy about something* in the agreement, either the fact that they've signed papers, that they put you to some expense, etc. Use this to keep them closed.)

"Can you hold a minute, Mr. Jones? I want to run into the office and try to catch those papers before they go in the mail." (Then I lay the phone down, without giving him a chance to ask what I mean. I let him wait a full three or four minutes, knowing the "papers in the mail" and his own conscience are working in my favor.)

"Mr. Jones, I was about 30 seconds too late. (Not, 'He was too late calling,' but 'I was too late,' which gives him an out; lets him accept the deal after all, and it's *my* fault.) The papers and cards are in the mail to the factory you know, the warranty, and all, and once they're mailed, there's no way in the world...gosh, I'm sorry, Mr. Jones, but I'll tell you what I'll do. When you come for the car remind me to fill it up with gas. That's the least I can do after I..."

There will be an isolated case where the buyer will be telling the truth; where something *has* come up that makes it impossible for him to honor the deal. When this happens, accept it gracefully and he might come back to you when he can buy.

In most cases, where he is simply trying to back out, the above approach will keep him sold and make him honor the deal he made

There are many other twists, any of which will get the job done that can be applied to the basic conscience system of avoiding prospect backout. Invent your own method, but keep *guilty con science* as your basic weapon.

I'm Sorry, He's Gone for the Day

Another very effective conscience rebuttal to the backout

attempt is to *do nothing*. The backout attempt is just like anything else the person might feel guilty about, and the sooner he gets it off his chest, tells the party or parties concerned, the better he feels about it. Conversely, the longer it takes him to unburden himself, the less he's going to feel like going through with it when the time comes.

I am never available immediately after a close. I might close the deal in the early morning, but as soon as the buyer leaves, the word goes out that I'm gone, as far as he's concerned, for the rest of the day, and probably tomorrow as well.

If it's a situation where the prospect can come to me, I keep an eye out for him, especially for four hours following the close, that being the time most buyers begin to have their second thoughts about the agreement.

If he tries to leave a message to the effect that he is backing out the receptionist politely tells him she can't take messages regarding a sale; that the management has found that it leads to mistakes, as the person taking the message is not always familiar with the details of the sale.

No Messages

Sometimes the prospect, feeling a bit more bold and determined with a third party than he would with the salesman, will *insist* upon leaving a message. When this happens, I simply don't get the message, "This is a very busy place, Mr. Jones, and that girl isn't the smartest in the world," until he delivers it to me in person.

The object is for him to have to stew over his decision, his conscience working for me again, for as long as possible. I have had the buyer get in touch with me and then not even repeat the backout message that I had told him I didn't get. He would change the message entirely, because his *conscience had made him decide to honor the deal after all.*

Remember that in the attempted backout situation, *time* is one of your strongest allies. The longer you can hold off his saying that he wants out, the less likely he's going to be to say it at all.

What Seems to Be the Trouble?

Another method of handling the customer backout is by means

of *simple persuasion,* plus a bit of authority. In the initial close you had to persuade the prospect to take the goods or service, so in combating the attempted backout you simply employ the same persuasion you used at the close, but with the added pressure of a double-team, *with authority.*

Of course you only use the double-team in cases where you didn't need to use it at the original close. If you used it then, the prospect may be expecting it, and have his defenses set up before the double-team can be put into effect, causing it to lose much of its persuasive power.

Remember, he is suffering from *guilty conscience,* and will want to get the backout over as soon as he can, with as little fanfare as possible.

He is not expecting to be confronted by a higher-up, one of the bosses, or someone with *more authority than you.* He feels he can handle you, but when you bring in Mr. Stevens and introduce him, you're telling him in a subtle way that you and the company aren't taking his backout lying down.

A carefully plotted double-team is even more important here than in the original closing. The man you team with *must* have a *detailed rundown* on what he is going to be up against, and a good *insight into the prospect's personality* so that he can decide upon the best way to handle him, to persuade him to go ahead and honor the deal.

No matter what approach he takes, the good double-team man will adopt a reserved attitude when he goes in to talk to the backout prospect. He will take his time about getting to him, and will leave his warm, friendly approach outside. He'll be polite, but *cool.* The time, as much as ten or fifteen minutes for the prospect to stew in his own conscience, will help to soften the prospect, and his coolness will show that he is not going to take kindly to an attempted backout.

You have, of course, told your partner everything he needs to know, but he will often go in as if he knows nothing about the prospect or his reason for wanting to cancel the deal. In this way he can make the buyer go back over the reason(s) for wanting to renege, and add to his discomfort over this unfair decision to back out.

Once he has let the man have his say and has heard the reasons for the cancellation, he can begin to combat it (again, he's very cool) by letting his attitude get it across to the prospect that he doesn't approve of his failure to honor a deal the company's representative made in good faith.

Standard Double-Team

At one sales agency where I worked we had a standard approach to double-teaming a backout, with the partner letting, just as in the sales approach, the prospect assume he had more authority than the salesman. Then, very slowly and methodically, he goes back over the transaction, step-by-step, letting the man's conscience do the work for him.

"Mr. Jones, I'm Reilly. Les here tells me there's some sort of difficulty with the agreement you and he wrapped up this afternoon. (Notice the subtle reminder that he made an *agreement* and it is *wrapped up.*) What seems to be the trouble, Mr. Jones?"

"Well, you see, Mr. Reilly, when I got home, I got to thinking about the payment, you know? (The closer is looking at him, his face stern but not frowning, and not acknowledging the fact that he can hear Jones talking.)

"When I got home and went over the contract, I got worried about those payments, and. . ."

Here the closer demonstrates his "authority":

"Les, how many times have I told you to go over the details of these contracts before your customer signs them? You know my rules about that, and you should have. . ."

"Oh, he went over them with me, Mr. Reilly, it's just that. . ."

"I see. Well, then, you *were aware* of what you were signing? Mr. Jones, I'll fire a salesman who tries to dupe our buyers (Buyers!) or get them to sign a contract which they don't understand. I will not put up with it!" (Slight emphasis on the "were aware" of what you were signing, another reminder that he made a deal in good faith, and that he knew what was going on.)

"Now, Les, did you figure Mr. Jones' budget to be sure that he could handle this payment? No matter, let's go over it again. I want him to be sure he can handle the agreement (Agreement!). What is your salary, Mr. Jones?"

The way this double-team expert is handling Jones, poor Jones is going to decide to go ahead with the contract, because he is being reminded, subtly, repeatedly, that *he made a deal.*

Coupled with this, the partner is going back over the same tracks that got the close in the first place. These two things working together with his guilt feeling should wrap the prospect up again with no more talk of backing out.

Depending upon how much of the transaction has been completed he may still be able to *force* the buyer into taking the product or service, if necessary.

The Last Day

Another effective back-in method using persuasion is the "This-is-the-Last-Day" approach.

This method can be used equally well with a double-team or by the salesman alone, depending upon the circumstances.

In simple terms, the salesman works on the customer's *sympathy* and persuades him to honor the deal for his, the salesman's, sake.

He can tell him that today is the last day of a contest and that with this sale he won a trip to Las Vegas, but that he *must get it in today* or he will lose to Joe Gibbons: he and Gibbons are tied for the lead and the contest closes, (he looks at his watch) in fifteen minutes.

I remember one fellow I double-teamed for a salesman I was training. The new man came to me to ask for help with a backout. The man had told him he had decided to wait a while and buy a boating rig that winter when prices came down.

Once we were seated in my office and Tommy had introduced me to his prospect I started with the regular, subtle, "You-made-a-deal-and-you-should-honor-it," but it didn't work. This man had decided that he was going to wait, and nothing I said would move him. I learned later that a friend had told him to wait until the off-season and he would help him get a good deal.

Then we played our ace card. "Tommy, I'm sorry. You did your best, and it's a shame for you to miss winning the first sales contest you've been in since you came with the company, but there will be others. Anyway, you gave it a good try." Tommy took my lead:

"Boss, the thing I hate more than losing that trip to Vegas is the fact that Mr. Jones here won't *ever be able to get this deal again* during the off-season or any other time. Of course that trip would have been nice, too. My wife was really thrilled."

"Uh, what kind of a trip? What's this contest you're talking about? Did the deal I signed mean you won a contest?"

We had him. I knew when he mentioned the deal he had signed that his conscience was working on him, and that he felt guilty about letting his friend talk him into doing something nobody with a conscience wants to do, back out of a bargain once they've agreed to it.

That and the fact that he discovered that his meanness was costing Tommy the top prize in his first sales contest would have made him go ahead if the lake in which he was going to run the boat had suddenly gone dry. It didn't hurt that he was getting a good deal, either.

"Yes, sir. You see the contest rules say a sale can be counted as soon as the *buyer signs the contract,* because that usually means he's sincere and few people will back out after they sign a contract," Tommy said. (How's *that* for a subtle reminder?)

He took the boat rig, and to keep everybody happy we threw in a pair of safety cushions and fifty feet of nylon bow rope at a total cost to us of about five dollars that we figured was well spent.

Feet to the Fire

There is one more way to kill a backout, but it must be handled by someone *in authority,* it being a last resort measure that can backfire. That is the "Hold His Feet to the Fire" approach, meaning *make him stick to his deal.*

When a customer accepts a contract and allows all of the papers to be signed and processed, he has, for all intents and purposes, *bought* the product or service for which he contracted, especially if he *accepts delivery.*

When all of the other methods of getting him to honor the deal on an amicable basis have failed, the person or persons in charge have to decide what to do.

They can let him go, and tear everything up, sacrificing the lost time, labor, and expense incurred in getting the sale, or they can get tough and "hold his feet to the fire." They can hold him to the agreement he made, even to the extent of going to court if the sale is large enough to justify it. However, this *must* be by company authorities, and for two reasons: first, the prospect may not bluff into taking the product or service under the threat of a possible lawsuit, and second, if he doesn't, it will be *up to them* to go ahead or withdraw.

Also, when the customer is forced into honoring his deal, he is going to be an unhappy buyer, and may be so hard to please in the future that it won't be worth the trouble it will cause to make him honor his agreement.

In any case it cannot be emphasized too strongly that this is a *situation for management,* and should be handled entirely by them. This is not to say that the salesman should let the prospect go without a struggle, or without taking him to management for a decision, but it is the owner or manager's decision whether to use the "Hold His Feet to the Fire" approach or not.

Be Prepared

Watch for the backout. It is during the close that the clues indicating an imminent backout will appear.

When they *do* show up, be prepared to cope with them. Use the *two safeguards* against the backout to attempt to head it off before it happens. If they don't work, be ready to employ one of the other methods designed to keep the sale in the "Closed" file.

Remember, there are two basic safeguards to be used at the close to insure against attempted prospect backout: first, *do all of the paper work* you possibly can, and second, *deliver as soon as possible.*

In the event these fail and you're faced with an attempted backout, employ any of the methods revealed in this chapter to combat it, using any version of your own that you can devise.

Regardless of the way you use it, the most powerful anti-backout weapon you have is your *customer's own conscience.* Use it to your advantage and your closes will stay closed. Fail to be prepared, or fail to employ a *planned backout defense* and you'll spend too much of your time tearing up contracts.

8

Six Closing Errors:
How to Recognize and Avoid Them

Six Guaranteed Ways to Lose the Sale

Just as there are certain things the salesman must *do* to insure a smooth and lasting close, there are things he must *never do*. There are mistakes he can make that will virtually *guarantee the loss of the sale*, wasting all his efforts and time.

Some will tempt the salesman as rebuttals to the prospect's objections, some will show up as "panic" counter-measures when the prospect says he wants to shop, and still others are the result of the salesman allowing the conversation to get on a personal level. All must be avoided if you are to maintain a high closing average.

One simple way to train yourself to watch for the pitfalls is to picture the sales talk as a long, winding road. You and the prospect are standing at the starting point, and somewhere in the distance, around many detours and curves, is the goal, the close.

Picture yourself setting out on that road with your prospect, and keep it in mind as your sales approach progresses. You will see and slow down for the curves, and detour around the obstacles.

You're Wrong, Mr. Jones. . .

Nobody likes to be told, even in a nice way, that he is wrong, and the thing we despise the most is to be *shown* that we're wrong. If it's simply another person's opinion, we can live with it, even though we resent it. But to be *shown* we're wrong is one thing we all resent and that resentment in a prospect can lead to trouble in closing a sale.

I went with Tommy, a new salesman, to help him close a local pharmacist on a $4,000 camper. He had a new pickup truck, and our firm carried a side line of quality truck campers. Tommy felt that he was close to a sale with the druggist, and asked me to go along in case he ran into difficulty.

We found his prospect in a receptive mood, ready to do business, and it looked like a simple matter of wrapping up the paper work and getting his check. As it turned out, it wasn't that simple.

His was a large store, the drug counter stretched across the back, with the druggist on a raised platform behind the counter. As we stood waiting for him to get a free moment, a man walked up and asked him how to get to Highway 11.

"Yes, sir, it's very simple. Go out to the highway in front of the store. Go left through three stop lights, and take a left. Go four blocks and you'll see a sign on your left indicating Highway 11 to the right. Now, don't get alarmed when you don't come to it right away. It's about eight or nine. . ."

Tommy interrupted the druggist, "Mr. Jones, there's a much simpler way to get there. He can go down to Grove Road, which is a half mile, take a left, and then three blocks to the intersection of Grove Road and Pine Avenue, and then. . ."

"Well, that *is* a little shorter, but I think he might get lost trying to remember the name of the roads. . ."

"No, sir. That's the simplest way. Here, let me draw you a little map, sir. I live on Highway 11, and I know. . ."

Later, when the druggist had dealt with his customers, he came down to the front where we were waiting and told us that he had decided to look at a couple of other campers before he went ahead and that he would be in touch with us later.

Nothing could change his mind. No matter how Tommy and I tried, he was adamant. He was determined to look at the other campers before he bought and had *changed his attitude completely.*

Jones Was Not Wrong—Tommy Was

On the way back to the office, Tommy was crestfallen and

dejected.

"I don't understand it. I had that man ready to buy, and all of a sudden he changed his mind. And that isn't fair. He had no business leading me along, letting me think. . ."

Tommy was new to sales, so I decided to let him learn his lesson then, preventing him from falling into the same trap again.

"Tommy, he didn't lead you on and then change his mind. You *handled* it badly. You lost that sale *yourself.* You, and nobody else, blew it. You were wrong, and when we get back to the office, I'll show where you violated a *basic principle of good salesmanship.*"

"What did I do? He changed his. . ."

"When we get to the office, Tommy."

He brooded all the way back, his chin on his chest, muttering about the "dirty trick" the druggist had pulled on him. When we got there I took him into my office and sat him down.

"Tommy, what was your reaction to my telling you that it was *your* fault that the sale was lost; that *you* were wrong? Now, be truthful, and tell me exactly how you felt."

"Well, I didn't like it. I was mad at the druggist, and then at you for suggesting that it was my fault. It wasn't, you know."

"We'll get to that. You were angry, right? You were angry at him, but most important, you were hot with me. You were hot because I said you lost the sale; because I said that *you were wrong.* Right?"

"Well, yes, but what. . .?"

"Tommy, think back. What did *you* tell *the druggist?* What did *you* say to him when you showed the man a simpler way to find Highway 11?"

"I just showed him. . ."

"What did you tell the druggist, Tommy?"

"I told him. . .he. . .was. . .*wrong,* and he got mad at me and did the only thing he could to get even. He refused to take the camper until he shopped. He was *showing me* that although he might have been *wrong* about the directions he would have the *last laugh by not buying* from me. . .me and my big mouth!"

Keep Your Opinions to Yourself

The next "don't" is somewhat akin to the "don't argue," and is even more apt to lose the sale, especially at the close, when the prospect is likely to be skittish.

Nobody likes to have their pet project criticized, or their favorite opinion disagreed with. This I learned the hard way, losing a large order and a profit of more than one thousand dollars.

I had the franchise for a storage battery that out-performed any on the market. It was unconditionally guaranteed, with a no-cost replacement clause, and demonstrations proved it to be twice what my competition could offer.

I had been to the local Naval Base, where they used thousands of batteries in boats, cranes, government vehicles, etc. The purchasing agent for the supply department told me to install one in each of four of their units, and that if they held up for three months he would give me an order for 1,000 of them, in all sizes. Government bidding is very competitive, but I stood to profit more than a thousand if the batteries help up, and I knew they would.

The three months up, the agent called and told me the batteries were going strong and showing no signs of failure, that if I would come by, he would get the order processed for the thousand he had promised.

As luck would have it the union was on strike at a local steel mill, and the papers were full of the reports of picketing, negotiations and minor violence at the mill.

While the agent went into another office to get the order processed I read the latest on the strike in the local paper. Then, assuming that he, being a member of the base management staff, would be against organized labor, I got ready to *really* clinch my sale.

When he got back I launched an attack on the unions and everything they represented.

He sat and listened. I told him they were always looking for a handout, that industry was at their mercy, and that the government (I *knew* this would get him on my side for good) should regulate labor, if necessary, to keep them in line.

At the end of my ten-minute discourse on labor-management problems he excused himself, saying, "Let me check on those papers. They should be ready by now."

In a few minutes he was back. "I'm sorry, but there was a minor regulation that I forgot about. You know how government red tape is. I'm afraid it will be a few days before we can complete this transaction, but I'll call you." I left, disgusted, but sure I had the sale, especially after taking the right stand in the union matter.

Wrong Stand—Lost Sale

A few days later I got a letter from the base. The purchasing agent regretted to inform me that due to "circumstances beyond his control" he would not, after all, be able to buy my batteries for base use.

I learned later that the base had contacted the factory and ordered the batteries direct, cutting me out of most of my profit. I had a franchise, so the factory had to pay me, but almost $600 went with the decision to buy direct. And I had to deliver and install the batteries.

I learned later that the government doesn't handle labor problems the way private industry does.

The board that listens to grievances, for government employees are not allowed to strike, was comprised of three members representing labor and three management, with a Navy officer presiding. But one of the *labor representatives* had to be selected *from the ranks of management,* and guess who that was? Right.

Remember, I had not been asked for an opinion. It was voluntary, and it was a mistake. The mistake lay in *offering the opinion* in the first place, and not in being on the wrong side.

Nobody had asked what I thought, and probably could have cared less, so if I had simply kept my opinions to myself, or expressed ignorance of the issues had I been asked, I would have been home free.

Discussing the situation with a shipyard worker much later, I found that the suggestion to purchase direct was probably offered by the agent's supervisor, and was probably not the agent's idea at all. But he probably could have argued in favor of doing business with the local franchise-holder if he chose to, which he obviously chose not to do.

The Right Stand Can Help at a Close

It is true that sometimes an opinion, the right opinion, can help at the close. I recall a time that we, several salesmen, were arguing about the best life insurance, mutual or the stockholder type. Tim had taken the position that the mutual companies were the best because the policyholders owned the company. He was very strong in his conviction that they were the best. But he knew when to switch, the sign of a real salesman.

"Mr. Jones, you sell insurance as an independent agent. Which is the best, a mutual or a stockholder company? That is, from the policyholder's view point," Tim asked a prospect who came in during the argument.

"There's no two ways about it. The stockholder company benefits will beat the mutual company every time, at a lower premium, and with more coverage."

"Hah! You see? *I was right.* And Mr. Jones here sells insurance for a living."

"But, Tim, you said. . ." One of the salesmen started to correct him but he hustled his prospect away and into his office.

When Jones left Tim came back out where we were still arguing about insurance.

"Tim, you're a rogue," the same salesman, a new man, said. "You argued for half an hour in favor of mutual insurance, and then when your prospect said stockholder policies were the best *you agreed with him.* Why, Tim? Why don't you stick to one argument or the other, or stay out of it altogether?"

Tim did a dance step and pulled his wallet out of his back pocket. He waved a sheaf of twenties at the boy and started for the office to turn the money in. It was a deposit.

"That, my boy, is why I changed my mind, for Mr. Jones, anyway. You didn't expect me to *disagree* with him, did you? And when I got him in the office, he was eating out of my hand, because I *had considered him an authority,* the last word, and then had agreed with his opinion. Salesmanship, son, salesmanship."

This was a case where the opinion Tim expressed, albeit he didn't agree with Jones one bit, helped him to get a close. But it only helped because Tim was wise enough *to get Jones' opinion first,* and then *agree with him.*

For the most part, it is best, and safest, to *keep your opinions to yourself.* They might backfire and cost you a sale, especially *at the close.*

Don't Marry Him

A sales manager told this story:

"Once upon a time two men were courting the same girl. She couldn't decide between the two, both being handsome, wealthy, sober men. So she made it a contest.

"She said that she would give each of them an hour in which to persuade her to marry him, and that at the end of that hour she would make her decision.

"The first suitor spent the hour telling her about his rival's escapades with other girls, his wildness and his extravagant living. Not a word about himself, or of his love for her.

"The second suitor spent the hour confessing that he had courted many other girls, but none was as lovely or desirable as she. He told her of his extravagance, saying that it was nothing compared to the extravagance he would lavish on her if she would marry him. He told her of his failures, of his sins, and begged for her hand, saying, 'You and only you can make me be the good man and good husband I want to be.'

"Whom did she marry? Three guesses. He told her that she was the *most desirable* he had found in all his searching; he told her that he would spend his money and his efforts to make her happy, and he told her that she was the only woman who could keep him straight. All the things she *wanted to hear!*"

The point is clear. You are there to sell your product, *not* to knock the competition. Continued emphasis on the short-comings of the competitor's product or service only accomplishes two things, both of them harmful. First it *focuses attention on that product* or service, and second, it *doesn't say anything good for yours.*

Another harmful result of spending your time knocking your competition is the "backlash" effect it can have. It is natural for the human animal to take the side of the downtrodden, to defend the oppressed, and that is just what your competitor is when you berate him or his product when he isn't there to defend himself. You might very well drive your prospect to see *the competition and his product for himself.* At best you're running the risk of alienating yourself with the prospect.

At your next sales meeting, suggest that the group try these fictitious sales talks and see which one sounds good, and which one sounds like trouble. Discuss them both, and get suggestions as to which is the best way to handle competition.

The "Knock the Competition" Close

"Mr. Jones, if you're ready to close this deal out you can just sign right here and I'll. . ."

"I thought I might take a look at the new line of tractors that Perkins and Company is advertising on sale this week. I understand they have a pretty good. . ."

"Mr. Jones, I don't mean to interrupt, but well, frankly, you understood wrong. (Wrong!) Sure, they're advertising them at a special price; it's the only way that that crook Perkins can sell anything. Why, you ought to talk to the people who have been in here telling us about the shameful way Perkins cons his customers into buying, and then when that second-rate stuff that he peddles falls apart they can't get him to look at it, much less come out and fix it. Shameful!"

"Second-rate? Why, I always thought Branson products were top of the line. I'm surprised. Say he's a crook, eh, son?"

That was all this salesman needed to really warm up on Perkins.

"Sir, if you walk out of here and go to Perkins you're going to make the biggest mistake you ever made in your life (daring him to do just that!), and then it will be *too late for us to help you.* Why, they tell me that Perkins and his sales staff. . .," on and on, until the prospect is sick of hearing it.

"Well, if he's that big a thief, I think I'll just mosey over there and give him a chance to cheat me. I've had a little experience with this sort of thing, and I'll get the price I want and make him do what he agrees to do in the bargain. See you, son."

"Mr. Jones! Mr. Jones. . .?" He's gone, straight to Perkins, and when Perkins hears how the salesman knocked him and his products, he'll get the sale if he has to *give* Jones the tractor, to teach the salesman a lesson, if nothing else.

How does this sound?

Agree As You Disagree

"Mr. Jones, this is the tractor for you, so you just sign right here on this line while I get the other papers together."

"Well, I thought I would check with Perkins and Company

before I decide definitely. They have their tractors on sale this week I understand, so maybe I should. . ."

"Mr. Jones, Branson products are very good. They build reliable equipment, and Perkins is an honest, responsible businessman. But he doesn't have the Power-Master line, and after all, it is rated number one by all of the top consumer publications in the country. True, he's having a sale this week, but they don't have the in-the-field service and repair feature that we offer.

"I am not knocking Perkins or his product, but when did you ever hear of them going on the job, free of charge, to service one of their machines? Mr. Jones, when you get ready to take in a crop, you *need your tractors.* You can't wait for help if one of them needs attention, and with us help is only a phone call away. Now, sign right here and I'll get the. . ."

"Rated number one by all the books, eh, son? Didn't know they rated them at all, much less putting Power-Master at the top. That's good to hear. Always want the best in my business. Good to have a good service policy, too. Hand me that pen, and let's get this over with."

Don't Knock His; Sell Yours

The second salesman got the sale for two reasons: he didn't try to convince the prospect the competition was junk; didn't spent his time knocking the other dealer.

And, he *did* spend the time *selling his product,* with facts, and with sensible arguments. In passing he even conceded (telling Jones in a subtle way that his judgment was good) that the Branson tractor was a "good" one, and that the dealer was honest and upright.

But while he was *conceding* he was *making a point for his product, and for his dealership.* His tractor was number one while Branson was "good." Perkins was an honest dealer while his dealer had a free service policy.

This is just as in the story about the two men wooing the same girl; one sold himself while the other knocked his competition, and the girl married the one who sold her on his intention to make her happy; whose claim that she was the only woman for him was what she *wanted to hear.*

She was not interested in how low-down the other man was, but in what *each man had to offer* her as a prospective husband.

The salesman selling tractors did the same thing. Rather than concentrate on pulling his competitor down, he *sold his product and his dealership,* being *fair to the competition* in the process.

Don't Play "Boss" Unless You Are

Every company, no matter how large or small, no matter what the nature of its business, has rules for its salesmen to follow. These rules establish the lines of authority, or command, if you prefer, and are designed to *place authority where it belongs.*

If every salesman, office girl, and clerk in the firm is allowed to make decisions as to company policy and procedure, the result would be chaos. Everyone would have a different idea as to the best way to handle a given situation, and there would be *no policy or pattern* for anyone to follow.

The wise salesman, for his own good, as well as that of his company, learns the company's policy and the chain of command. Then he *never ignores the chain or varies the policy.*

The primary reason for sticking to company policy is to *avoid making commitments that you çan't keep,* or *making decisions that aren't yours to make.*

What can, and usually does, happen when you attempt to alter or interpret company policy?

Assume Authority and Lose the Sale

Nathan was an insurance salesman, and a good one. He had a friend who played linebacker for a professional football team, and when his friend came home for two days one Christmas, Nathan sold him a large life insurance policy.

There were no restrictions due to his playing football, but the company had a mandatory physical examination clause, regardless of the applicant's age or condition. Nathan had been with his company for many years, and knew better, but because his friend told him he had to leave town that day, Nathan accepted a letter from the team doctor in lieu of an examination.

His friend was driving back to his team when he crossed the

highway center line and ran head-on into a tractor-trailer. He was killed instantly and the insurance company had to settle the double indemnity policy at $100,000 because Nathan had accepted the team doctor's letter which put the policy in effect until the company either accepted or rejected the application.

A subsequent investigation revealed that the man had suffered from chronic double vision which didn't affect his playing football, as he was a lineman, and sharp vision was unimportant, but it could have, and probably did, cause the accident.

The Payoff

Nathan lost his job and found it impossible, at 54, to get another sales position. The last I heard he was working in an insurance office as a clerk, checking applications for $100 a week.

Nathan had committed the unforgiveable sin by interpreting his company's policy, not the way he knew it to be for many years, but in the way he felt it should be. More than that, he had failed to let someone in authority rule. They might very well have decided that the letter could be accepted anyway, and he would have been in the clear on an important matter.

Always the Boss

At all times during the sales approach, *follow the chain of command.* Your supervisors are supervisors for a reason, be it special talents, experience, years of service, or what. Even if you feel that a supervisor is incompetent, remember the old saying; he may not be always right, but he *is* always the boss.

Nathan's mistake was disastrous because it appeared at the close, and he lost more than the sale as a result. So did his company. He took it upon himself not only to ignore authority, but also to go against, attempt to change, the established policy of his agency.

When matters of authority or policy crop up, especially during the close, where they can make the most difference between a sale and a no-sale, *don't take chances.* Get an interpretation *from management;* you won't lose the sale by telling your prospect something wrong, and you'll keep your bosses happy.

The Deadly Tendency to Oversell

Many salesmen, when they come in contact with an easy sale, make a serious mistake. They *oversell*, because the prospect is gullible or easily sold.

The tendency is not only unfair to the prospect, but can have disastrous after-effects for the salesman and his company. He has an obligation as a legitimate and ethical salesman to fit the product or service to his customer, and there is an important reason for not over-selling that will affect him personally. A sale the salesman knows might rebound on him or his company is not a sale at all. A sale motivated purely by greed is not a sale. A sale made under shady or double-talk circumstances is not a sale. All of the above are *problems, not sales.*

Left Shoe on the Right Foot

Dick met the elderly woman as she came through the door into the showroom and asked to see a four-door sedan with automatic transmission. One of the other salesmen recognized her and told Dick that she was wealthy; that she was the widow of a real estate man who had owned several apartment buildings and a dozen houses he rented, in addition to having been the most active rental agent in the city.

There was one problem however: there wasn't an automatic transmission four-door on the place. All they had was a four-door with a big V-8 engine and a floor-shift four-speed transmission. It had been ordered by mistake, and the sales manager had put a one hundred and fifty-dollar flat commission on it.

Dick took his prospect out to the four-speed, showed it to her and told her that as the Korean War was going on, all the automatic transmission automobiles were going to the military.

He reminded her that she had learned to drive with a floor-shift, saying that it would come back to her, and that "it will give you less trouble than the automatic, and it's three hundred dollars cheaper."

He was a smooth talker and a convincing salesman, and she let him talk her into taking the four-speed. This was against the advice of two other salesmen who tried to remind him that a truck load of automatics was on the way and would probably be in within the next two or three days. Dick argued that she was in her right mind, she had the money, and besides, pay day was the next day and he needed to get the sale in before cutoff.

The old lady managed to get off the lot, gears clashing, and Dick gloated, contemplating his windfall. Two weeks later her lawyer called.

Again, the Payoff

He allowed to the manager of the dealership that his client was capable, that she allowed herself to be sold the car, and that they had no grounds for a lawsuit.

He said that he had simply called to read a paid advertisement that he was going to run in the local paper the next week. It stated the terms of the sale, with all of the pertinent facts. Nothing criticizing the dealer or his salesman, just what had happened. That the salesman had told her the military was taking the automatics, that the engine was a souped-up three-hundred and fifty horsepower, and the other facts, including his client's age. It was signed by the purchaser, and the paper had agreed, because it stated the facts without complaint or criticism, to print it starting the next week.

The dealer couldn't afford to let the letter be run in the paper, and his conscience wouldn't let him anyway. Instead, he called Dick into his office, asked him whether the letter was true, and discovering that it was, fired him.

He called the attorney and told him he would take the car back, delivering any car that the lady wished to buy. Lacking that, he would refund her money in full. He also offered her five hundred dollars for her trouble and her sworn statement that she was satisfied.

She refused the money, saying she did not wish to do any further business with that dealer. She only wanted her money back, and would sign nothing.

The Consequences

The car was brought back with two fenders damaged, for she said that she couldn't depress the heavy duty brake pedal, and more than a thousand miles registered on the odometer. She told them her nephew had put it on at her insistence.

The dealer weighed the consequences of trying to fight, gave her the money back, and had a used, damaged car on the lot with more money in it than he could ever hope to get back.

Dick had gotten the sale, and had probably done the best job of his career at the close. But what did he accomplish? He lost a good job and a good commission, and went a step further in insuring that the time would come when no legitimate dealer would let him work his lot.

When you get to a close, *tell the truth,* and sell your prospect the *product or service he needs* and the one that will *fit his particular circumstances best.* That way you will get a chance to close him again, and you should get a chance at his friends and family because you did your job honestly and legitimately.

There is another oversell pitfall that many salesmen fall into which is equally dangerous.

When you're selling financed contracts or insurance where there will be a monthly payment, *don't oversell your customer on payments.* It may put more money in your pocket at the moment, but you will earn a reputation as an over-seller, one whose deals cause collection problems or cancellations, and before long you'll be in trouble.

Reviewing the Don'ts

For an effective, lasting, and trouble-free close, remember the Don'ts: *Don't* argue with your prospect; *Don't* offer your opinions or criticise your prospects; *Don't* knock your competition; *Don't* assume authority or break the chain of command; *Don't* oversell your product or the finance terms; and most important of all, *Don't* ever succumb to one of the other five "don'ts" believing that, "Just this once won't hurt," or, "The DONT'S really didn't apply in this case."

This is step number one in falling into the habit of being less than an honest and straightforward salesman; the beginning of the end for a good closer.

The man who can't see past the end of his nose, the fellow who thinks only about closing that sale today, now, will ignore these helpful suggestions—no these helpful *"musts"*—and go on his merry way.

Then, one day he'll look around and discover that he's standing alone, with no following he can depend upon, or that can depend on him, and worst of all, that his company's confidence in him is destroyed.

9

The Four Basic Buyer Types:
How to Close Them and
Keep Them Closed

Most salesmen habitually classify buyer types by personality and/or the extent of their sales resistance; the strength of their "brick overcoat."

This is well and good, but there is a better and simpler method of grouping buyer types that will simplify the sales approach and smooth the rough spots out of the close; make it possible to deliver more prospects and keep them delivered.

Most of the salesmen on whom I tried this were skeptical at first, both the old-timers and the newcomers. They felt that it was too general; that the prospect couldn't be classified on such general terms.

Then, when they had used this approach they learned that it does what it's designed to do; it leads to an effective, lasting Big League close in the least amount of time with the least effort on the part of the salesman.

The Key

The key to grouping prospective buyers lies in two words: *circumstances* and *confidence*.

Take a sheet of paper and list 25 prospect types: a married bricklayer, a single schoolteacher, a married lawyer, a divorced truck driver, and so forth.

At first glance most of the 25 will appear to be different, but they can be accurately grouped into one of four categories, and they will conform to the limits and probabilities of that category.

The Four Groups

Generally, the *professional buyer*, the *family buyer*, the *individual* and the *unattached female* will appear over and over in your list of 25, and each will fall *within one of those four groups.* Individual circumstances will apply within the group, but all will be subject to the pressures and influences of *that group. Circumstances peculiar to that general group* are half the key to closing them, and keeping them closed.

The other half of the key is *confidence,* the age-old necessity for an effective close. We all know the importance of gaining the confidence of the prospect, especially at the all-important close.

So the complete key to the effective close from a take-them-as-they-come approach is: *group the prospect where he belongs, and apply the rules of that group* to *gain his confidence.*

Closing the Professional Buyer

What about the people who buy for their living just as you sell for yours? The fellows who know all the tricks of making you cut your price or move the delivery date up to get the sale; of playing you against your competition; of utilizing every mistake you make to make you sweat. They know how to make you panic into selling short, or promising a delivery date you can't meet at a profit.

The key to gaining their confidence is to *be prepared.* Don't *you* be so naive, or expect *him* to be, that you simply walk in, show the professional some statistics tailored to make your product look good, and ask for the sale.

Don't make the mistake of thinking that a steak dinner or a night on the town will get you the order. He'll eat your steak and drink your company's whiskey; then he'll give the order to the man who has *shown* him what he needs to see; *proved* to him that *his* dump trucks can do the job, or shown him that *his* plant can have the steel or concrete at the site on time.

Close Him with Facts

This buyer *must* be, will *demand,* to be *shown.* He isn't buying upholstery colors or barbecue pits or double indemnity clauses. He's buying *facts, and only facts.*

He knows that you can produce statistics and pour them into his ear, but they will more than likely run right out the other. He wants to *see for himself,* he has been *told* too many times.

We are agreed that the professional buyer knows the tricks of buying. But he knows the tricks of selling even better. He is more than likely an ex-salesman, or has at least had dealings with the best the sales field has to offer, and at least feels he has done a good job for his company. If his company officials didn't think so, too, he wouldn't be a purchasing agent.

Close him by using the one thing that makes him different from other prospects: his *knowledge of salesmanship and buying.* Sell him *facts, hard prices* and, where possible, *demonstration* of the product or service.

The cute sales pitch, the well-turned phrase, the, "I-like-that-tie," approach are going to leave him cold. His time is valuable, to him and to his company, and he is going to want you to spend that time selling him on your product or service, not flattering him or sweet-talking him.

Know Your Business

Take a straight, to-the-point, no-nonsense approach, *know what you're talking about,* and close your share of the pro buyers.

"Mr. Gregg, I'm Joe Perry of Amalgamated Steel Company. How are you, sir? Mr. Gregg, my firm would like to figure with you on the steel for the Acme Office Building. We knew you folks were low bidder because we had a bid in too."

"Yes. Well, if your company had a bid in you know we probably made a mistake by bidding it too low. I don't see how they figure I can buy steel. . ."

Stay One Step Ahead

"Yes, sir. I know what you mean, and that's where I come in.

You see, my company keeps the sales and engineering teams working on these bids from start to finish. Then, if we don't get the bid, our sales staff is familiar with the specs and requirements and we're able to work with the successful bidder, providing the steel at a minimum cost to him."

"Your firm is headquartered in St. Louis, right?"

"Yes, sir. But we already have 70 percent of the steel in a warehouse here, five miles from where we're sitting, in case we had gotten the bid. And since we didn't, we can supply the steel to the low bidder."

"Good thinking. Was that your idea, Perry?"

Do Your Homework

"No, sir, it wasn't my idea, but let me show you what was. See right here, where they specified the 10 inch, I-beam supports? More than ninety-five tons of steel, Mr. Gregg. We entered a note with our bid (I think you got us on labor, we being from out of town), requesting permission to use these special, welded angles, back to back, in place of the I-beams, and they're 13 percent cheaper. That's a lot of money, Mr. Gregg, and it's a welding job a second-year apprentice can do with some simple jigs. . ."

"You say it's 13 percent cheaper, eh, Joe? Say, that could be a big help. . .we really cut the bid on this one to the. . .let's see that spec report. . .yes, it could work. You say they approved it in your bid? I think I'll show this to. . ."

This salesman got a big order for steel because he had *done his homework.* He knew the steel business, and had made it his business to familiarize himself with the very project for which the purchasing agent was getting ready to buy steel. By being in a position to *talk specs,* and show the agent a cost-saver, he was home free, with a sale.

Sell the Newcomer

In this example, had the purchasing agent called in an engineer to consult with him, the salesman would have immediately shifted the sales pressure to the engineer, the man who would handle the steel work. By getting him on his side, the salesman would have made his job much easier.

"Mr. Spell, I've drawn up some simple jigs that will show you our thinking. Now, you're an engineer, and I'm not, but as I told Mr. Gregg here, these beams could be welded up of the angles back-to-back, and including welding time, rods and overhead they can save you about 13 percent on the total cost of the framework. They'd be lighter and seven percent stronger, too. Help to keep the inspectors happy, eh, Mr. Spell?"

"Gregg, he's got something here. Matter of fact, I was thinking along the same lines, wondering whether we could do something like this. . ."

When there is more than one purchasing agent or authority whose opinion is going to matter, or in a case such as the one above, put the emphasis, provided you have convinced one or more of the buyers, on the newcomer. Tell him in an offhand way that you've sold them, line him up on your side, and the close will be easy and smooth.

Closing the pro can be summed up in one simple statement: remember that he is *a professional buyer.* He probably was a salesman at one time, and you must assume that he was a good one, one who knows the tricks.

You must assume that he knows his business. He knows what his company needs and wants, and he knows how to go about getting it. He wants *facts, demonstrations,* and *proof* that yours is the best service or produce he can buy for the least money.

Few of the tricks of the trade will apply to him. *Facts, demonstration,* and a *convincing, persuasive sales talk* will get the job done. Lies, half-truths, and veiled promises will get you nothing.

Closing the Individual

It might be wise to jump all the way across the buyer market from the professional to the rank beginner, the youngster, to point up the advantage of closing each prospect within *his own group.*

In the professional you encountered very little true sales resistance, because he has learned not to let "I want," or emotion affect his purchases. He's all business, and he knows what this leads to; he only buys what he or his firm needs, and only when they need it.

The newcomer to the buyer market, the young fellow buying

his first car, insurance policy, boat, or home, might very well represent the *highest level of sales resistance you will ever encounter.*

They may not be with him when he encounters the salesman, but his parents, his wife or girl friend, his friends, or even his employer have told him to be careful. They've told him that all salesmen will try to take advantage of him. They've told him to shop all of the places that sell the commodity for which he's looking. They've told him to check prices, financing, warranty clauses, fine print, and the degree of shiftiness of the salesman's appearance. They've told him so often that he's frightened half to death.

His brick overcoat has been assembled carefully, and tightly mortared by the well-intended people of his acquaintance; so much so that he's terrified, expecting to be skinned alive by the first salesman he meets.

This very fear, this feeling that you're out to con him, is going to make the close simple if you follow the rules that apply to the newcomer.

Gaining His Confidence

His fear, his brick overcoat, have shown what you must do: *gain his confidence.* Show him that his fears are unfounded, and that the advice he's been getting is *all wrong.* Once you have accomplished this, and it can be deceptively easy, you're home free and he'll be a cinch to close.

A word of caution: the same "don'ts" mentioned in the last chapter apply to him, only more so. Remember, this is a newcomer, a green buyer expecting to get fleeced, and if you so much as utter a wrong word you're going to lose him.

The brick overcoat the new buyer wears will be made of one of two types of brick. He will be the loud-voiced, "you-can't-kid-me-because-I've-been-warned" type, or the "I'm-going-to-go-slow-and-look-at-each-detail-minutely-so-you-can't-take-advantage-of-me" prospect.

The first will be inclined to talk louder than normal; might even be rude, if not downright obnoxious. He will show his fright by trying to play the tough guy, the fellow who's been around.

His youth and his tough-guy attitude are the tipoff, so don't let them worry or upset you. Let him talk, swagger, and tell you about how well informed he is; that he's going to be a hard sell. The more he talks the more relaxed he's going to get; the more he's going to begin to doubt that this thing of buying something he needs is going to get him hurt; especially if you're calm, agreeable, and not shoving him toward a close.

Identify

Once he's had a chance to let off some of the tension (this may take considerable time, but it pays to let him do it), you begin to *identify with him*. Identifying with him is the key to removing his brick overcoat. When *you* identify with *him*, or conversely, when *you let him* identify with *you*, you'll rapidly gain his confidence.

Suppose you're in the 40 to 50 age bracket, and he's in the 18 to 28 range. There's your identification area. You are the same age as his father, or at least in the same range.

Find out the relationship between him and his father, or, if his father is deceased, find out who his "father image" is. It may be an uncle, his employer, or just a family friend, but there is usually an older person he looks up to; one he trusts and respects.

When you have found out who that man is and what his relationship is with your prospect, *identify* with *that person*. Sometime during his display of bravado he's going to drop the clue, without realizing he has. "My dad told me how to handle you salesmen," or, "The boss told me about you guys selling cars," will be the tipoff. He wouldn't mention that person unless he trusted him; unless he paid attention to that person's advice.

Once you know who it is, pick at him for the advice he received. What did that person tell him? What was that person's opinion? What did he tell the prospect to watch for? Then it's simple: agree with the adviser and *prove* that the adviser gave him the *right idea;* the *best advice he could get.*

". . .and uncle Fred said that I should investigate the possibility of placing the emphasis on savings and loan companies; that the way this area is growing I couldn't go wrong. . ."

"Mr. Bailey. (*Don't* call him Tommy unless he asks you to. Most of the youngsters' fright, their sales resistance, is based on their youthfulness and inexperience, and getting too familiar only emphasizes it.) Your uncle sounds like a smart man. You're lucky to have him to advise you. Is he in business, or retired, or. . .?"

"He's a colonel in the Air Force, and he has an investment program that he started when he was about my age. He knows how to buy, how to get up a sound investment folio. He also knows how to keep from getting taken. . ."

"Sure he does, and like I said, *you're lucky.* Now, I believe it will be best to go back over the things he covered in telling you about the savings and loan investment, to be sure you understand what he meant. I'm sure he showed you this. . ."

"Hey, you know, that's *exactly* what uncle Fred said. That I should put about 40 percent of my inheritance from my father in. . .you know, your brokerage was one of the ones he recommended, too. I think I feel better about it, now. You know, someone who thinks as he does, what with his being successful and satisfied with *his* program over the years. . ."

The bravado, the fear, is rapidly dissolving because the salesman *identified with this young man's adviser,* his uncle, found out enough about the uncle to guess at his investment attitude and experience. He will soon have the confidence he needs to remove the bricks and go for a close on an investment package.

The Quiet, Soft-Spoken Show-Me Type

This young fellow usually has no adviser he trusts, so he lets his *fear* of making a mistake slow him down, cause him to measure each word carefully, and examine each detail.

The key here is to be sure you're on the right track by asking him whether he has someone to go to for advice. It can be done in many ways, but the simplest is to ask him point-blank, "Who do you ask for advice in important matters like this, Mr. Bailey?"

"Well, actually, I don't have anyone. Of course, there's mother, but she doesn't know anything about investments. In fact, this is for both of us, our inheritance from dad, and she's depending on me to. . ."

"You know, that's a coincidence. My brother died about three years ago, leaving a daughter about your age, and his wife. He had a few thousand in insurance and savings, and they asked me to set up their investment program.

Fill the Void

"Frankly, I was a bit reluctant at first. You know, them being my family, and all. And then I said, 'No, if I can't do the job for them, and get them the best I can, who can I do it for? I should get out if I can do it every day for strangers and then don't trust myself with my own family.'

"I set them up like this. . .and then some really blue chip growth stocks. . .and it's working out fine for them. . .now, Mr. Bailey, would you like for me to. . .?"

"Uh, why don't you call me Tommy, sir? I mean, you're old enough to be my father, and I think we're going to be doing business. . ."

In dealing with the youngster, *gain his confidence.* Whether his brick overcoat is made up of "advice" bricks, or "caution" bricks, gain his confidence and the close will be easier, smoother.

One fringe benefit to be had by gaining his confidence will be two-fold, for once the young person has done his buying successfully, he invariably becomes an "expert," and will send his friends to you, *the man he trusts.*

Also, he is young, so you will have his business the balance of his life; and as he grows older and moves up the income ladder his *business with you* should *increase. DON'T abuse or betray* that hard-won *confidence.*

The Experienced Individual

The other half of the individual group is the older, more experienced person who is not the head of a family, not a professional, and has to please and provide for only himself.

This being the case, why does he fall in the same buyer-market-group with the newcomer? Because although he's an individual and has only himself to answer to, he still *listens to someone.*

Here again we must remember that this person is on his own, and that we need only gain *his* confidence; we need not worry about his, "Let me talk it over with my wife," or, "Let me show the figures to my partner," but we might have to contend with an adviser.

We must also bear in mind that we must work even harder to

gain his confidence. He is not a beginner, not gullible, and certainly not easily sold until we show him that ours is the best for him.

He is in the individual group, he makes his own decisions, but he too, just like the newcomer, takes or at least considers, somebody's *advice*, so the key to this individual, again like the newcomer is to discover who that person is and his relationship with the prospect. Then identify with that person.

It's Really None of My Business, But. . .

We had just broken up a sales meeting when Dick caught a prospect that fit the subject we had discussed. We had talked about the fellow who brought his adviser with him to help him do his buying, and the best way to handle the situation.

Dick was a new man, and I know now that the adviser proposition frightened him because we had discussed the fact that he, the adviser, was often a know-it-all, big-mouth whose sole interest in the deal was to shoot his mouth off and ridicule the salesman at every opportunity.

Unfortunately for Dick, we hadn't had time to discuss the way of handling the adviser type, so he was understandably jittery when the next prospect he caught had his boss with him.

It *was* fortunate in that he got a first hand lesson in handling the adviser, and a lesson in closing the experienced individual by identifying with the person he consulted, in this case his employer.

Dick called me in when the adviser insisted repeatedly that "It's none of my business, Adams, but I think you should look around. . ."

I went into the closing room, introduced myself, and explained that Dick was a new salesman, that he was in training, and that we usually helped with their sales for the first few weeks.

"Mr. Adams, you're interested in this four-door here, the one with the automatic transmission and small V-8, right?"

"That's right, but I think Mr. Pearson might be right. Maybe I should look some before I buy."

I turned to Pearson. "Mr. Pearson, it sounds to me like you know this buying business, especially with cars, where a fellow is spending a lot of money and can easily make a mistake. Mr. Adams is lucky to have you to advise him."

"Well, it's none of my business, but. . ."

"Don't feel that way, Mr. Pearson. I meant it. You know you

business, and you're willing to help your. . .are you fellows just friends, or. . .?"

"Adams works for me."

"Well. So much the better. If he's satisfied with the way you treat him as an employee he knows you won't fool him with the important advice on buying a car.

"Now, Mr. Pearson, what do you think of the deal we've offered? Do you think it's fair? And please don't say it's none of your business, because it is. You owe it to your friend and employee, Mr. Adams, to give him the best advice you can, just as we owe it to him and to you to see to it that he gets the best possible buy for his money."

"Well, since you put it that way, I would say that if you were to shave that figure a bit more and throw in a set of white-walls. . ."

In most cases, the close, from that point forward, will be a matter of finding the common ground, the right price or product, and wrapping up the sale.

The prospect had shown that he usually takes the boss's advice, probably thanks to good, sound advice that paid off. This being obvious, say so. Throw in a little flattery, concentrate on the adviser, and the close will be simple.

When the experienced individual buyer comes in contact with the salesman alone, it's even easier to find out who he listens to. Praise or identify with that person, and watch the bricks fall out of the coat. The individual who never consults anyone in his circle of friends, acquaintances or family, is rare indeed. It is a simple matter of discovering who that person is, what their advice was, and concentrating on *pleasing* or *identifying with them*. The rest is easy.

Closing the Unattached Female

Every salesman, consciously or not, has his favorite among the types of prospects he meets in the course of a day. Mine is the female, unmarried and self-supporting, regardless of her age.

You will notice that I have grouped this person in a separate category by herself, and there is a reason. Although she falls into the general individual group, she is a separate and distinct, and valuable prospect many salesmen shy away from, which is a mistake.

The woman who does her own buying with nobody but herself

to please or accommodate is the one prospect the salesman can really *sell*. Being a woman, she is susceptible to every trick known to the sales profession, and, depending upon the individual circumstances and her personality, she can be a pleasure to close.

She is susceptible to flattery, can't resist beauty, is sympathetic, and rarely is forceful. The real beauty part of selling the woman lies in one trait every woman has. Young or old, married or single, wealthy or not, she *rarely knows what she needs or wants.*

Selling the woman can be a salesman's delight. He can run the gamut with her. He can analyze her needs and her likes, and with a dab of flattery here, some good, practical advice there, having her eating out of his hand in no time.

A friend of mine recently opened a travel agency in a large city where there is a tremendous vacation travel market among the young, working girls.

"In this business I meet all kinds, but I concentrate on the working girls who have to get the most for their pay, and maybe a few dollars they've saved, so I keep this in mind.

"Some want to visit a glamorous place, where they can meet young men and have fun. Others, the intellectual types, are thinking in terms of ancient history or the arts, and they feel just as strongly about their wants as do the girls looking for the eligible bachelor.

"What I really enjoy is that I can *sell* these women. I use all the tools of salesmanship at one point or another, and still being fair and honest, give them the most for their money.

"With me, selling them, especially at the close, is a real chance to sharpen my salesmanship, because although you can use all the tricks, few of them are pushovers when it comes to spending their money and their two weeks. They want flattery, yes. They want glamour, yes. They want to be told they'll have fun.

"But what they *really* want is to *be able to trust what I tell them.* They want to know I'm looking out for them because they don't have a husband, father, or boy friend to tell them what's best. This way I've built a six-figure business, and I enjoy every minute of it."

The Family Prospect

Perhaps the largest group in the buyer's market is that of the family buyer. He's the head of his household, and every large purchase is his responsibility.

Of course he probably will, for the most part, consult with his wife in most matters, but the ultimate decision will be his. He might discuss the size of the new stove they need, or the location of the new dryer or the amount and type of life insurance he is going to take out, but there it ends. When the decision is made, the man of the house will more than likely make it, and stand responsible for the outcome.

This is not to say that the rest of the family should be left out. The wife and children will have their say, and although they don't make the decision, they certainly influence it. It is a shortsighted salesman who doesn't try to sell them along with the father.

Many salesmen carry this approach even further and concentrate on whatever member of the family will be most affected by the purchase. For example, going back to the dryer, the woman of the house is going to use it the most, so it is often wise to emphasize the ease of loading, the automatic cycling and the built-in lint collector to her. The easy payments, trouble-free performance, and the warranty or breakdown insurance can be left to the man.

Split the Family Up

Many times it is wise, especially where there are teenagers, to sell the new family car or boat to the children, and the financing, safety and maintenance to the parents.

Here you are placing the emphasis on the member(s) of the family who will be most apt to help you get the sale by joining forces with you when you move in for the close.

It is a rare man indeed who can resist the pleas of a pair of teenagers telling him, "Daddy, the vinyl interior and bucket seats are the greatest," or, "Dad, that single-control eighty is a sweet running motor, especially on that Bluestreak 18 footer."

Where do you think father is going to be when his wife says, "I know we can't afford it, but that four-burner gas stove with the copper hood and the automatic, self-cleaning oven is really beautiful. . .and so practical."

How many fellows have been able to resist *that* kind of talk from their wives or youngsters? Very few, or theirs are different from mine. Remember this: a man lives and works and struggles for his family; to do for them, to keep them happy, and to preserve their happiness, whether he admits it or not.

Sell a Member of the Family

One author of several books on salesmanship breaks the family down into "commodities." He said the man should be sold the insurance, the stocks and bonds, the hospitalization, and things of that nature. In most families he is the provider and the worrier, so he is best prepared and will have the most to say about the important items.

The wife should be sold the furniture, the appliances, and the other items that are primarily for the house or yard.

The boat, the car, the swimming pool, the so-called "luxury items" should be sold to the children and the wife, and the home to the entire family. Selling the luxury items can be a great deal easier if one feature is sold to the children, another, the one that appeals to her more than any other member of the family, to the wife, and the man of the house the practical aspects of the deal like the financing and price.

A friend of mine gave me a step-by-step briefing on the method he used to close a family on a new home in a better neighborhood after the man of the house had been promoted.

He met the family at their home, which was paid for, where he had been sent to discuss a larger home. They wanted, "one in the same neighborhood, and not too much of a price increase over the one we own. I don't feel up to taking on another mortgage at 56."

He told them about a new listing he had in a fashionable new development on the outskirts of the city, telling the man that he knew he probably wouldn't be interested, but that he just wanted him to see it in case he knew someone who might be. He had waited until they were in his car headed for the area.

When they arrived at the house he didn't say anything about price, payment, or insurance. He took the 17-year-old and showed him the tennis court at the back, and then showed the daughter, 15, the kidney-shaped pool and cabana.

He took the mother inside and showed her the laundry room, the maid's quarters, and the all-stainless kitchen with the hooded stove and huge freezer.

Having seen a large collection of books scattered all over the old house in bookcases and on shelves, he showed the man the den, with its walls lined with bookshelves and the picture window overlooking the canyon.

Every time the man said, "It's really nice, but too much for us." the salesman agreed, reminding them that he wanted them to see it just in case. . .

Then he took them to the house they had talked about. It was nice, and well within their budget, but it didn't have a tennis court, although there was one at the high school in the next block.

It didn't have a swimming pool, either, but there was one at the school. It didn't have a powder room or a deep freeze, and the stove wasn't new, but it was convenient to the high school and the bus stop.

Each Member Helped at the Close

The entire family, including the man, was sold, but not on the second house. They had seen what they wanted, and it was a simple matter of easing into a closing situation by suggesting that it wouldn't hurt to get an appraisal on their old house and a trade price.

The father's misgivings and fears were dissolved by the excited squeals of the daughter and the son's comment about the "keen" basketball court he could set up at one end of the tennis court.

Of course the wife's speculations about how much meat she could get in the freezer didn't hurt, and the thought of moving into an "executive" neightborhood was an exciting prospect for the man, who obviously felt that he had "arrived."

In selling the family the luxury items, leave the financing and technical planning to the man, and sell the rest of the family on the features that will appeal to them most.

Dealing with insurance, investments, and things the wife and children have no knowledge of, or interest in, concentrate on the man and his obligation to the rest of the family.

In short, if you separate the family according to the commodity or service you're selling, but at the same time hold them together and concentrate on the fact that they are a family, the close will be easier.

The basics apply in all four of the buyer types. You must have their *confidence*, you must *identify* and you must *place them in the proper grouping* to make the close easy.

Analyze their circumstances and *place* them in one of the four groups. Then decide where they fall within that group. Next, *build their confidence* in you according to their individual type. Last, *identify* with them or with the person they turn to for advice, and the Big League close will come as naturally as telling them to "Sign here."

10

Let the Customer Work for You: How to Prospect at the Close

An age-old rule of selling is, "You don't get the sale until you ask for it."

To paraphrase that old saying, "You don't get the *prospect* until you ask."

This was and is the key to the most successful and long-lasting sales streak I have ever witnessed; simply asking for the next prospect *at the close.*

Failure

Fifteen years ago, Fred, a used automobile dealer in my home town, went broke. He will tell you that when he closed his lot he was in debt, and didn't have a dime to his name, since he had been wiped out by his creditors.

He had a wife and two sons to support, house payments to make, and all of the other bills a family man has; but he wasn't licked.

He sat down and analyzed his circumstances and decided that he was not a businessman. He was not suited to running his own business because he had too many friends and was too soft-hearted to make it in the rough-and-tumble of the business world.

He decided that because he had friends, and because he was a good salesman, he was going to stay in the automobile business as a

155

salesman for someone else. He also planned the strategy that was to make him one of the *top used car salesmen in the United States.* The amazing part of his strategy is that it is so deceptively simple. Fred told me it has *three major points,* and that application of those three points at every contact, at every close, has put him where he is today.

Identity—Prospecting—Reminder

"The two main points are *identity* and *prospecting.* The third is a *reminder* that the other two must always be uppermost in my mind *at the close.* I must *identify* with that buyer, and I must *ask for those prospects.*

"I decided when I went broke to put all that behind me and become the best salesman in the United States, and although I won't say that I'm the best, I will say that I get my share of sales.

"I realized that as a salesman I needed something to make people think of me when they got ready to buy, and that I had to have prospects while I waited for those who already knew me to contact me. In a nutshell, I needed a *reminder for the old prospects,* and I needed to *meet the new ones.*

"It took me a long time to figure out how I was going to accomplish this, but after looking at it from all sides—I wanted something inexpensive, simple and foolproof—I hit on the solution.

"First, *identity.* I bought a dozen felt derbies at a local men's shop and dyed them a bright green. Then I ordered my cards, with the company name and phone number, and my new slogan, 'Ask for the Little Fat Man in the Green Derby.'

"I wore that derby, and do now, everywhere I went; to lunch, to visit prospects, to the barber shop. The guys I work with accuse me of wearing it to bed, and if it would help identify me, I'd do that, too.

"Of course, the object was to identify me with the used car business, and also to remind people to ask for 'the man in the green derby',....me. I figured that my name was one that most people would forget, or that they would misplace my card, but I knew they'd never forget that derby and the little fat guy under it; and they haven't."

Prospecting

Let's digress for a moment and look at his success. Fred's expensive home is paid for, and has been for years. He has put one son in business, three new, modern liquor stores, and another through a major college.

He owns property all over town and recently sold an apartment building, which he built, for a six-figure price, and now he is considering an apartment complex that might conceivably go into seven figures. *All on the income of a used car salesman.*

"Fred, you say your *identity* and your *prospecting* are the two main points in your success. I know how you identify, but what about prospecting?

"Do you mail postcards, make cold telephone calls, that sort of thing, or. . .?"

"Are you kidding? The day I have to make cold phone calls or write postcards I'll hang up my green derby and quit. No, my prospects come to me *at the close."*

"At the close?"

"Right. Look, when I have just wrapped up a sale, I have already gotten the best future prospect there is, the man I just sold. Why hit him once and drop him? If he lives he's going to buy again, isn't he? Why should I let him go somewhere else when he's ready to buy again?"

"What do you do, then, at the close, to insure that you'll get him again?"

"First I lay it on the line. I ask him whether he's satisfied with the deal I got for him, and with the car I sold him. This will work for the fellow selling insurance, real estate, or mutual funds, as well as to the hardgoods man.

"If he says he's happy, fine. If there is something still bugging him, then I get that out of the way first. I want him to say, and mean, that I'm a nice guy; a guy who treated him fairly, and got him the best possible deal."

"And then. . .?"

"Then I tell him, not in so many words, but I get it across to him, that he owes me. He owes me the names of two or three people who are ready, or soon will be ready, to buy a car.

The Key to Live Prospects

"I say that this is the key for a good reason: push him into it and he'll give you a couple of names that aren't worth calling. You could do better calling cold from the phone book.

"The key is that I get it across to him that I am going to expect him to give me *legitimate, bona fide prospects* who are going to buy, and soon.

"I refuse to let him tell me that he doesn't know any, because I have proved too many times that he does, whether he realizes it or not.

"It may be his neighbor, someone he works with, his family (there's a great source of prospects), the man he rides to work with, his pastor; the list is endless. Someone he knows, and this is a mathematical fact, is going to buy a car, insurance, a washer, house, or what-have-you within the next 48 hours."

"Okay. You get the names, and of course you follow them up by telephone or in person, right?"

"In person. *Always in person.* And here's where identity comes in. Lots of people have asked me if I don't feel silly, a man almost 60, wearing a kelly green derby everywhere I go, but it's my *identity*, and I don't feel silly, especially when people come in and say, 'I have forgotten his name, but they call him The Man in the Green Hat.' "

"Fred, do you mean to tell me you never do any other sort of prospecting? Like watching the wedding announcements and the graduation ceremonies, that sort of thing, for prospects?"

He laughed. "I might try that if I ever get caught up with the prospects I get at the close, but judging from my files, I'll be a hundred years doing that, and I plan to retire before then."

Three Musts

My talk with Fred revealed three things about this very successful salesman: he *maintained his individual identity,* he did virtually *all his prospecting at the close,* and he *made his prospecting contacts in person,* so they would have the lasting affect he needed to stay successful.

Fred's aversion to cold phone calls and mailing postcards is well-founded and understandable, for a program that depends upon this sort of hit-or-miss prospecting is worse than no program at all.

The salesman who does this would be better off if he went to the local coffee shop and sat there, waiting for someone to offer to buy from him. At least this would be a lead of sorts, because someone who knew he was a salesman might ask him to sell them whatever it is he sells.

Harry sells as many shoes as any member of the company's sales team. He's married, has five children, and he sells shoes from his automobile for a very good living in five figures; all this in spite of the fact that he's disabled.

"When I close a sale it leads straight to the next one, no stops and no detours; *straight to the next sale.*

"Hey—there's an idea for a slogan for my card—"You're next." Anyway, what I just said is true.

The Prospect Chain

"I'm 62, and had a coronary three years ago. I was a mediocre $7,600-$8,000 a year road man for a chemical firm, but I had to retire. Now I spend three or four hours a day, five days a week, making about $12,000 a year. Funny, isn't it, that I had to learn to sell when it was almost too late?

"I found the secret, the 'open sesame,' in one simple statement, my current record of consecutive sales is 56 and I'm going for more. 'Mr. Jones, I just sold your friend (brother-in-law, neighbor, boss, etc.) two pairs of these (I have a shoe in my hand, and give it to him) shoes, and he suggested that you might be interested in some.

'We have a sale on this week, and if you order two pairs now, I can really give you a good price. Notice the workmanship, Mr. Jones, and the quality of that leather .

'Oh, by the way, I've sold (again, the friend, neighbor, some lawyer he knows, etc.) several pairs of these shoes, and his whole family is wearing them now. Calls me his traveling shoe store.' "

It is a *never-ending chain,* one customer referring him to another, the trick being to mention the *last two* who have done business with him when he approaches the new prospect.

The new prospect knows those last two customers, and it makes it a great deal easier to sell if Harry can tell him they do business with him.

Never Stop Closing

The proof of Harry's success? While we talked he took a beautiful cordovan wing-tip out of his case and handed it to me. When he left, he had a deposit and signed order for two pairs, one of the wing-tips, and one of a pig skin loafer, to be mailed to my home C.O.D.

Coincidence or Proof?

While we were talking he mentioned, as he eased the sample out of his case, that he had sold some of his specialty, golf shoes, to Fred, the "Man in the Green Derby." I called Fred before I started this chapter. "I bought the shoes from Harry several years ago, and have bought several pairs since."

And Fred said he buys all his shoes from him, and that several of the other men at his dealership are also Harry's customers.

Harry uses the last sale to bridge the gap to the next one, and when he gets there, he refers to that sale to help him make the next one, and so on. This is *not a coincidence*. It is the *proof of Harry's prospecting system*.

Ask yourself this question: how many consecutive orders have *you* gotten, by having one customer refer you to the next? You might try another question while you're at it: do you prospect at the close? If the answer to the first is not many, then the answer to the second is obvious.

Imagination Pays Off

I was having lunch with a sales manager friend of mine when we got on the subject of prospecting. He said, "I will fire a salesman of mine who depends on cold telephone calls or mailing postcards to get his prospects."

"Okay, so you'll fire the man who makes cold calls. What *is* your secret? What do you advise as the best prospecting plan for your men?"

"The salesman who's on the job should never be without at

least two hot prospects at all times, but when they *do* get low, he can use the telephone, without calling cold.

"How, then?"

"I'll show you when we get back to my office. I'll pick out a folder on one of my low producers, a man I am afraid I'm going to have to let go, and show you why he's falling down. He could be a good salesman, too, but he's always whining that he doesn't have prospects, and I can't sell houses that way."

Back at the office he pulled the file on the last sale the man had closed; a clean deal, all the loose ends wrapped up, a neat profit on the transaction, and a good commission for himself.

My friend made a note of the old address of the buyer, and got out a city voter registration list. He looked up several nearby names. Then he looked up their telephone numbers and picked up the phone.

When he had finished ten minutes later he had picked up the fact that one of the neighbors had talked to the new buyer's wife, as they were good friends, and that they were also considering moving into the new subdivision in which their friends had just bought. They had *not been contacted* by anyone from my friend's firm. There was a sale *right in front* of the salesman *at the close,* and he ignored it, or simply didn't realize that *the next sale is more often than not right there at the close.*

This aspect of prospecting at the close is part of *identity.* You *establish your identity* by referring back to the last sale, to a person both of you know, and when you leave that person you've just closed, you *take a name or two with you.*

And as you have just seen, the telephone can be invaluable if you *use your imagination* and your ingenuity, instead of wasting your time and efforts on cold contacts.

Sorry, Wrong Number—or Is It?

Some time when you have a few minutes to spare, try the, "Sorry, wrong number" phone prospecting approach, but *not cold.*

When you have completed the sale to Mr. Stevens, you will have his address and telephone number, and, if not, it's easy enough to look it up in the city's voter registration lists. Look up the number of the six closest neighbors, and call them, one at a time.

"Hello. This is Harry Borden, with Providence Insurance. May I speak to Mr. Stevens, please? I forgot to get his. . . ."

"I'm sorry, but you have the wrong number. This is the Green residence."

"Oh. . .well, that's funny. I didn't have Mr. Stevens' number. . .I handle his insurance program for him, you know, life insurance, the house, that sort of thing, and I looked his number up in the city directory. I have it right here in front of me. . .2136 Maple. . .I wonder where I made my mistake. . . ."

"This is Harold Green, Mr.. . .what did you say your name was?"

"Harry Borden, Mr. Green. With Providence Insurance on Walden Avenue. . ."

"Well, you see, this is 2137 Maple. Jim Stevens lives across the street. You say you handle his insurance? Funny he hasn't mentioned you. We fish together some, and he knows I need to talk to someone about. . ."

Of course this is not going to happen every time, but I'll guarantee you *four hot prospects* and *one sale* for *every six calls* you make, which is not bad in anybody's prospecting book. Also, I have never had anyone hang up on me or bawl me out like they often do on a cold call.

Use Your Ingenuity

Ed is a furniture salesman and he's smart. He's so smart that he always arranges to have the new couch or coffee table or dinette set delivered to the wrong address. That's right, the *wrong address*. It works like this:

When he has completed the sale and it's time for the delivery, he follows the truck in his car, "to be sure they get the right house." When the truck gets in the neighborhood he tells the crew on the truck (a dollar apiece helps, he says) to carry the couch, from which he has torn the protective covering—up to the house *next door* or *across the street* and to take the blanket off it while they wait for someone to answer the bell.

When they answer, and if he's lucky it will be the woman of the house, the delivery men act as if they have the right house and start inside with it. That's where Ed comes into the picture.

He gets out of the car and "realizes" that he has made a mistake, but also explains to the lady of the house that, "we're having a big furniture sale at Conlons, and Mrs. Perkins bought this beautiful couch, etc., etc." Unorthodox? Nervy? A miracle? Yes, and it sells furniture. Really, this is another *prospecting at the close* system.

It would take thousands of words to describe the various pet approaches to prospecting at the close that have already been devised, and more than that to try to cover those that have yet to be tried.

Two Fundamental Truths

Use your imagination, and invest your own methods, but do remember that your most fertile prospecting ground is found at and immediately following the close.

When a man learns a trade he picks up certain basic fundamentals that apply to any job he tackles. They are truths which play a part in every project related to his trade, and he always uses them.

If your trade is that of salesman, then just like the plumber, there are basic fundamentals of your business that you have learned; that you *always apply to the close.*

Identifying yourself speaks for itself. If the prospect remembers you, you'll get a chance at his business; if not, forget it. If you've lost a finger on one hand, show it to the prospect when you leave him. If you're a redhead, remind your prospect that you are; if you're the world's worst bowler, put it on your card and make a point of telling everyone you are. *Identifying is one chance* to survive in the competitive world you're selling in.

Your other chance, and equally as important as identifying, is *prospecting* as we all know. But don't write postcards that might net ten replies per thousand; don't take numbers out of the phone book; don't wait for the prospect to come to you; instead, ask for them *when you close a sale.*

The buyer is in a receptive mood at the sale. You have just helped him accomplish something that he's probably wanted to do for a long time. Take advantage of it while he's feeling congenial.

He has probably discussed this buy with someone in the last few days or hours and that someone is your best chance for your next sale. Ask for his name and address and permission to use your customer's name.

I Dare You

A *challenge* and a *promise:* go back over the last 20 sales you made, and list them. Then ask them, preferrably in person, for *three prospects each.* This would be a total of *60 new prospects* if they each gave you three. Assuming that they won't all be willing to give you three names, or that they aren't all able to think of three, let's be conservative and say that *you get 20.*

Those 20 prospects, properly contacted, in person if possible, will *guarantee you six hot prospects,* and *at least three sales.* Try it. I dare you.

Bear in mind that this is not prospecting at the close, where the possibilities are the best. Therefore when you get those six hot prospects and *close three of them,* just think about what you might have done had you asked for them at the original close.

Apply the technique of *prospecting at the close* and you'll never have to double back over your sales file—you'll be too busy closing sales and visiting new prospects.

11

Five Big League Guidelines for Effective Paper Work: How They Can Help You at the Close

The Solid Gold File Cabinet

Ted had sold appliances at a local store for more than twenty years, leading the board most of that time. There were eight men on the sales staff, and he was at or near the top month after month.

Upon retirement, he arranged for his son, who had just graduated from college, to take over his slot in the staff. Many of his friends were incredulous; why would Ted let his son, with a college degree, go to work as a *commission salesman* when he could have a salaried job paying much more?

I knew Ted and had known his son since he was a toddler. Right after Gary's graduation I stopped by the house, ostensibly to congratulate the boy, but actually to sate my curiousity.

While we drank coffee and made small talk the question kept popping back into my mind. Why did Ted let this boy take a job as an appliance salesman when he had a brand new degree in business administration?

When I couldn't stand it any longer I asked them, point blank, the question that everyone was asking. *Ted's reply was an eye-opener,* in more respects than one.

"When it came time for me and Gary's mother to select a

graduation present for him, I wanted it to be something more than a diamond ring or a new car, either of which we could afford. We talked it over, and agreed that the best place for Gary to prepare himself for business management would be at the bottom, *where the business originates; as a salesman.*

"Then we agreed that our gift should be one that would *help him as a salesman* to help him get started and to see the *importance* of *the sales staff* in any business.

The Best Graduation Present a Student Ever Got

"Gary, get your graduation present and show it to him."

The youngster got up, went into another room, and came back carrying a large metal file cabinet. This was one of six that his father had filled in his career as a salesman.

He opened it and revealed dozens of manila folders, each neatly lettered with a name and address. Then he showed me the value of this file, the way his father had shown it to him.

In each division, A through Z, were the names of *every customer Ted had ever sold,* with detailed information about that customer and the sale.

Clipped to every name card was a slip of paper with the dollar commission that each sale had brought Ted. There were thousands of dollars worth of sales, all carefully recorded on the cards.

Then Ted had gone through the file and listed the potential, or hypothetical value, of that sales file.

In twenty years he had made sales of more than $2,000,000 and had earned commissions averaging more than $15,000 yearly. In addition, the file showed a potential over the next five years, if it was used properly, of more than $1,000,000 in gross sales.

As a sweetener, and to show the lad that his parents weren't trying to get by his graduation present cheaply, there was a hundred dollar bill in each letter divider—26 of them.

Gary was as enthusiastic as his parents were. "Look at this, sir; Dad has shown that the fine life we've enjoyed all these years has been a direct result of his *keeping this record file active* and *current.*

"Why, you can look through it and find the year we bought the cabin at the lake, the year Dad bought me my first car, and the year mother got her mink. It's all in there, in recorded sales. It's a regular gold mine if I use it right."

Glancing through this card file I saw the key to its success. It was a great deal more than the old, name, address and telephone number. It was a *sales file.*

Make the File Complete

The name, address and telephone numbers were there, but so were the place of employment, the prospect's occupation, and his time on the job, along with his salary.

The *names, sex, and ages of his children* were also there, along with a one-line description of each.

The record included when they bought appliances from Ted, what they paid, and how. There was a copy of *each contract,* and a note on the *easiest way to approach the couple at the close.* And there was much more.

Instead of a hit-or-miss card with only the essentials, Ted had a *composite file* on each person or couple he had ever sold, along with comments to remind him of how to sell them when they would be ready again, and data on their friends and relatives.

Gary took that file cabinet and installed it in his closing office at the store. For the first three years he out-sold his father, and then the files and his degree really paid off. They appointed him sales manager, on salary.

One of his duties was to train new men, so I asked him what was the single most important thing he told his new men with regard to keeping records. "That's easy," he said, "don't settle for a card file on your sales and prospects. A complete record of sales and the persons to whom the sales were made is the most valuable sales tool a man has. I tell them how Dad got me started.

"This is especially true *at the close,* because if nothing else the salesman can fill himself in on details and not have to ask questions as to how the prospect wants to finance, how many children he has, that sort of thing.

"When the customer sees that the salesman remembers him and his wife, and asks, 'By the way, how is your son, Tommy? He must be about ready for college, isn't he?' that customer is flattered. And that, to me, is what it's all about; make the close easier any way you can. That's the name of the game."

Remember: it only takes a few minutes more to *get all the*

facts; the facts that can and will help you in the future, whether it's another closing opportunity with the prospect listed, his son, his daughter, or brother-in-law.

Just as the time to ask for prospects is at the close when your customer is apt to be the most receptive, so is this the time to get the facts about him and his family for your file.

Ask him then about his job, his children, his relatives. Of course much of this information will come as a natural result of the close, especially in the financing situation (credit statement), but not always, and not always enough. When it doesn't come, *ask for it.*

Keep It Current

A major requirement of the file system, one that will make or break its effectiveness, is to keep it *current* and *up to date.* Again, it only takes a few minutes to go through the file and add or remove pertinent information as it applies. Also, the salesman who wants to make his file more comprehensive, or wants to improve its effectiveness, should add two active, live prospects to his file *every day.*

How, then, do you find those two new names when you don't make a sale every day, and how do you keep your files up to date?

Watch the Papers

The newspapers are a most valuable aid in keeping your files up to date, as well as a source of new names to add to your prospect files.

First, let's see how the papers can help you to keep the files current. Take an average man whose name, as a past customer, is in your files. Everything that happens to this man is, at one time or another, *recorded in the newspaper.* His daughter gets engaged, it appears on the society page. But the key to an effective and helpful file is to go a step beyond simply recording the fact that his daughter has gotten engaged.

When the marriage ceremony is performed, this will be the beginning of a new family, and you will have a foot in their door because the father, or father-in-law, is a customer. The daughter will probably remember you, too.

These items should be added to the father's file: the name of the child getting married, the date, who she is marrying, and if possible, their plans—where they'll live, etc.

When his daughter gets engaged, it's on the society page. If his son graduates from college, it's in the paper; he wins a scholarship, it's there; he leaves for the Army or comes back home, it's in the paper.

Let's take the hypothetical engagement announcement and see what to do about it.

The New File

Begin the file on the new couple. Their name, address, where he works, and all the facts that you can dig up about the new husband.

The proof of this being worth the trouble is simple; is your product or service normally used by newlyweds? You bet your life it is, and this includes a cemetery plot.

Just as asking for the prospect when you closed a sale (in the last chapter) led to more sales, you have just gained two brand new, live opportunities by spending a few minutes bringing the existing file up to date and starting a new one.

You have a bona fide excuse for calling the father and offering your congratulations. When you do this you are reminding him that you haven't forgotten him, and that you recognized his name as the father of the bride.

You have an opportunity to ask whether there is anything you can do for him and his wife, or for the new couple. And you can rest assured that the new couple is going to need appliances, life insurance, a house or apartment, groceries, clothing, and a thousand other things, one or more of which might be the service or product you sell.

The Company Newsletter

Don't overlook other publications that list promotions, births, and the other pertinent details about your prospects. They lead to new sales. The company publication, club periodicals, and church papers are all sources of these tidbits that will put sales in your record. Even though your files might contain hundreds of names after a few years, you'll find that you'll recognize the names in your files as they appear in the papers.

One very successful salesman I know keeps double files; one on *sales he has made,* and one *on potential sales.* The one on past sales is self-explanatory, while the one on future sales is made up of names and details from that file other than the customer himself.

For example, when his son graduates from high school, a file is begun, separate from the father's. The facts are then carefully recorded; where he goes to college, his military service, etc.

This file is maintained until the first sale is made, no matter how long it takes, even if the son might be listed in the files for years before the first sale is made. This is rarely the case anyway, because again, you have your "in" with the son through the father, and it usually isn't long before the son needs the services of the salesman, making him a hot prospect.

File the Family

This fellow, a life insurance salesman, also keeps files on the close relatives of the customer wherever he feels it might lead to a sale.

"I make as many sales to the young brothers-in-law and first cousins of my prospects as I do his own children and him," he said. "It's always easier (remember the shoe salesman?) to make the contact and get results when you have a personal referral, asking the new prospect to, 'Contact your Uncle Harry and ask him about me. I've handled his business for ten years.' "

Watch for the news items that affect or pertain to, your old customers. Don't overlook the company and church periodicals, and *keep your files up to date* so you'll know what's going on in your customers' families.

Public Records Should Be Called Goldmines

A newspaper reporter acquaintance of mine once gave me one of the most valuable record-keeping tips I have ever gotten.

I asked him how he verified the facts when he was doing a story. For example, he did a story about slum conditions in our city.

Where did he find out who owned the buildings? How did he know that the building inspectors had tried to get the owner to repair the building? How did he discover that the owner was the behind-the-scene owner of the Ace Realty Company, notorious for its rent-gouging tactics?

"Public records. Few people except lawyers, police, and news personnel realize that the term means exactly that: public records are the *property of the people,* and nobody has the right to refuse to let you see them. In fact, they are glad for you to do so, could care less about why you're interested, and will usually go out of their way to provide the answers you need."

This set me thinking. If they were open to the public (I was one of the people who thought they were privileged), wasn't there something I could do to supplement my live prospect file by taking advantage of this fact? There was.

Check the Court House

The records in the court house listed property owners, court actions (lawsuits, judgments, etc.), taxpayers (the property they pay taxes on and how much, including the value of the property), marriage records, and births. As it turns out, all of the facts about all of the people were in the files of the city and county offices.

Local State Highway Department records listed all of the automobiles registered in the county, with the make, year and the owner's name. (This is *gold* for you automobile men.)

Register of mesne conveyance listed real estate transactions as they occurred, and the tax books listed them back fifty years and more.

A trip to the marriage license office revealed that two of my old customers, one a bachelor getting married, and one a daughter of a customer, should be called for the possibility of further business.

Telephone company records, the water and gas departments, and public school records, have all led to good, sound prospects. How much time did these contacts take? Very little; one day a month devoted to checking the records paid off consistently, and will pay off for you.

How Old Is Your Company?

There is another excellent source of prospects that many

salesmen overlook. Some don't recognize the value of this prospect goldmine, while others simply discount its worth.

Suppose your company is a fairly new one, say ten to twenty years old. Even though it's young by most of the standards, whatever product you sell or service you offer there are records in the company files that *can mean more sales for you.*

It is an established fact that the turnover in sales jobs is very high. Some can't make it, some retire, others go on to higher jobs, but while they're with the company as salesmen they *make sales,* and *these sales are recorded* in the company files.

Once the man who made those sales has left the company, the repeat opportunities are fair game for the man willing to go after them. If that salesman did his job properly when he made the original sale, the customer was impressed enough that he might want to do business with the company again, or to suggest that his friends and family do business with them as well.

Even if he did a slipshod job of closing the sale, it can be a source of new business for you. In cases where the customer is not happy with his purchase or with the way in which it was handled, you can use this as a means of getting his future business for yourself by *offering to correct whatever it is that he feels isn't right,* and in that way *endear yourself to him.*

If that last salesman did a good job, so much the better. All you need do is contact the customer, tell him Sims is no longer with the company, and that he, Sims, asked you to take care of his accounts to be sure that they were happy and satisfied.

Suppose you're selling automobiles, for example. The office files always contain a copy of the order form and the sales contract. They are usually grouped together by the year in which the sale took place, so it is a simple matter to go back through them and pick out the likely ones.

The average person trades his car every third or at the latest, fourth year. Get the files out for the two years and go over them, picking out the ones who traded with a *high equity,* or who *paid cash.*

If the office manager is really sharp and on the ball, he will have made notes on that bill of sale, showing the customer's age, marital status, etc., which can be a great deal of help to you when you contact him to ask for another deal.

It is worth mentioning, too, that you support your efforts to keep up with your own past sales by referring to the office records periodically. You're bound to find some in there that you've forgotten or overlooked, and these can be of the utmost value to you as a salesman.

Check the company files. This will apply to every salesman, regardless of the type of merchandise or service he's selling, from hardgoods to mutual funds. As time goes by, every customer becomes a prospect *again and again*, and it is up to you to get your share of this *virtually captive business*.

The Legal Pad

Keeping permanent files and watching the company records for prospects is fine, but what about keeping track of the every day, working-now prospects? How should you stay abreast of those prospects you're dealing with now, that you're trying to close?

The best and simplest method I have been able to find is the legal pad, a long, yellow-papered pad for sale in drug stores and five-and-dimes. If you want to go first class the five-and-dime stocks a plastic folder that will protect the pad, keep it from getting stained and dog-eared.

The system I use is simple. As soon as I have talked to a likely prospect, his name and address are entered on the pad, leaving room for notes and a record of my progress with that prospect.

If I am to see or call him the next day, a note to that effect and the date goes on the pad. If he is coming up to me in three days, the same. In this way I don't lose track of him or forget him (*there's* a good way to lose a sale), and am constantly thinking about him, trying to figure how I can best close him now.

Keep a permanent file on every sale and every prospect. It is easier to file the names and addresses of some you may never *see* again than it is to forget or lose track of some you might *sell* again.

Ask for prospects at the close. Your customer will never be in a more receptive mood, and he has friends and family who are prospective business for you. Ask for their name and address at the close.

Watch the papers. They are a goldmine of prospect information.

And don't forget to keep your eye on the public records. They, too, can lead to more closing situations.

Remember to *check the company files* for the sales made by men who are no longer with the firm. At the same time you will come across sales you made and perhaps overlooked or forgot to enter in your permanent files.

Keep yourself current with your working prospects with a *running, at hand record of your everyday prospects.* This will keep you on top of the situation as it develops, and ready for the close when the time is right.

Remember: *the number of sales you make is directly proportional to the number of times you go for a close,* and the *miracle lies in identifying* and *prospecting.*

12

The Close Begins at the Opening:

How to Qualify for the Close

There are many important aspects of the sales approach that are directly related to the effectiveness of the Big League close. All are necessary and must be considered in the overall lead-up to the close, but there is one phase that is more important than the others, which must be dealt with accordingly lest all the rest be wasted. That all-important phase is *qualifying the prospect.*

You might have the best product or service money can buy, you may be the best and most persuasive salesman in the firm, and you may be a great closer; but if you aren't a skillful qualifier, then more than half of your deals will develop into no-sale situations. You will have wasted your time and effort in attempting to close a prospect who can't for one reason or another, be closed.

It Makes No Sense

You know from experience that there is nothing more difficult to explain to your sales manager than why you spent a day or more with a couple, showing them a $25,000 home, only to discover that the husband had been laid off the job a week before.

Or you talk to a young fellow, show him the boat or car he is interested in, see the government check for a thousand dollars in his shirt pocket, spend four hours demonstrating, and then have him say,

"I'll tell my father in California about this one," (you're in New York), "and ask him to sign for me. I'm only 18."

Time and *experience* are the two most valuable assets you have, so *apply them.* Use your time qualifying the prospect right at the start, before you get involved in a situation from which it is virtually impossible to escape without wasting more time.

Use your experience by applying principles learned in other closes that will bring out the problems so that you can solve each one as it arises.

You must qualify the prospect. You must have a 100 percent method of qualifying, and you must use that method with every prospect. This will insure that you don't lose possible sales because you didn't apply your qualifying plan or because you missed a clear sign that said, "It doesn't show on the surface, but this sale can be made."

Before we get into the actual qualifying techniques, let's look at some examples of what can happen when you fail to qualify, or when you don't do a complete job.

You Can't Qualify Sitting Down

It was early Saturday morning. We were sitting around the showroom, some of us reading the paper, some drinking coffee.

We were selling new and used automobiles, with a staff of ten men, all competing on equal footing. There was no split-shift or day off, and open floor from eight to seven, six days a week.

A young boy, a teenager, wandered onto the used car lot and began looking around. Louie, a fellow who had just come with us from an insurance debit, asked me if I wanted him.

I looked up, saw the kid, snorted something like "What for?" and went back to my paper.

Louie got up slowly, laughed, and said, "Well, I guess I can practice my sales pitch on him," and went outside.

Fifteen minutes later the boy had picked out the car he wanted, called his father, a local doctor, and rode with Louie to the father's office to get approval of the boy's choice and a check.

It was a short while after I learned this lesson in qualifying that the same thing happened again; only this time I was on the other end of the deal.

I caught a young prospect one morning. I qualified him very carefully, to be sure I had a prospect before I let him waste my time, or worse, let him get away.

Imagine my disgust when I asked him where he worked and he said that he had started with a local construction firm the first day of that week. When I asked him where he had been previously, and for how long, he really knocked me for a loop.

"There's no use to try to hide it, or fool you. I've been in the *penitentiary* for the past *31 months* for housebreaking. But I'm clean now, and I mean to stay that way. I need a car to get to and from work, and if I can get one I'll be all right."

"You've been in the. . .in jail? For 31 months? And you want to finance a *car?* Son, I'm sorry, but you. . .wait a minute. Let's see what we can do. Come into my office."

I had sworn I wasn't going to lose another deal because I failed to get all the facts, and caught myself just in time.

Everyone who heard the boy's story, in spite of the fact that he had a 40 percent down payment, scoffed and asked me whether I was crazy calling a deal in on a jailbird. All, that is, except one.

I called an acquaintance in the finance business and asked him, before he passed judgment on the deal, to talk to the fellow; see whether he might be tempted to give him a chance.

The boy got the car, the construction company now has the best construction superintendent it ever had, and my friend finances anything he wants because he's never missed a payment in more than ten years.

Six Basic Questions That Guarantee Sound Qualifying

Granted that you can't do a practical, foolproof job of qualifying from a distance, and that every prospect has to be qualified or potential sales will be lost, what is the best way to go about the qualifying?

Ask six basic questions, and, armed with the answers and your experience as salesmen, you can determine whether you have a "now" prospect, a "later" prospect, or a "never" prospect. You will *move in* for the close with the *first, file,* but *keep in touch* with the *second,* and *drop the latter.*

The questions:
1. Where does he (she) work and how long?
2. What does he do there?
3. Where does he live and how long? (Circumstances—own, rent, etc.?)
4. Marital status? Children?
5. Who is the (car, boat, insurance, furniture) for?
6. Appearance? (physical, speech, manner, attitude)

Each question, properly asked, will yield a wealth of information. Looking at each answer separately you'll learn to evaluate that answer in terms of its bearing on a possible sale, and also in terms of the answers to the other questions.

For example, the first question could apply to you, the salesman.

Suppose your prospect tells you he's an encyclopedia salesman and that he's been with his firm three years.

You know enough about direct selling to know that it's a hard game to succeed in. You also know that if he's made it in this field for three years, he must either be pretty good or a hard worker, or both. Why? You know they don't pay any salary, only draw against commissions, most of them, and to survive you have to produce, maybe more consistently than in any other sales field, and it's primarily door-bell punching.

On the negative side of this coin is the transient possibility. A great deal of these people are in a city for a few months and then move on to another. They may only come to your town once in two or three years.

This could indicate that financing might be a problem, depending on several other factors. But here you see that the answers to the other questions are going to tie into the first: where he lives, his marital status and whether he owns or rents his home may indicate that he is (or is not) a transient, and may still (or may not) be a bona fide prospect.

What does he do? This is another question that may reveal a great deal, as will be illustrated in a later example of how the answer to this one can affect the sales approach.

He might be a ten-year employee of the city, a notoriously low-paying job, but he might also be the man in charge of the public service commission, able to buy the company you work for if he chose.

The answer to question three, where he lives and whether he owns or rents, is important for many reasons. First, applying it to the encyclopedia salesman, he might tell us that he lives here, is buying his home, and does his traveling in other towns; that this is his firm's home base. He's a resident in spite of his traveling job. No problem getting financing with this one.

Or he says he lives 200 miles away, is single, and rents an apartment in what turns out to be a plush, exclusive apartment building catering to high-paid singles. He's had the apartment more than two years, and casually mentions that he has a five-year lease and is having his place redone this month. Again, no problem, probably. But get *all* of the answers before you decide.

Notice that the answer to the last question provided the answer, if he's truthful to the next one. Marital status and children. He said he's single, but has he *been* married? Is he supporting several children, a definite drain on his income? Is he away from home working to avoid the law, charged with non-support, or owing back alimony?

A good lead-in to explore this possibility could be, "Never been married, eh? Well, I don't blame you. I'm married, and happily, too, but then I'm older than you. Don't blame you for wanting to have some fun before you settle down.

"The guy I feel sorry for is the one who's divorced and has to maintain a wife and kids plus a separate household for himself. Must be murder at today's prices."

This will usually get the separated or divorced person talking, but don't let it kill the sale. I, just as you, have closed many divorced people, often with their ex-mate's approval, and once or twice with their help.

Why ask who the purchase is for? After all, if you get the sale, you couldn't care less who the car, furniture or other merchandise or service is for. Right? Not so.

How many times have you spent time with a prospect and then been told that he's shopping for his sister, his boss, or one of the fellows in the office? Plenty.

You can't, and you know from experience that this, too, is all too true, *sell something to one person for another.*

The Tough Ones

The one thing I dread more than anything else when I talk to a prospect is for him or her to bring an "expert" with him, one who knows more about the product or service I'm selling than I do. Nine chances out of ten he's going to knock everything I say, and try to demonstrate what a hotrod buyer he is, killing any chance I have of a sale.

The next thing on my hate list is the person who "heard Joe say he needed a new power mower so I thought while I was down town anyway I'd look at some for him." Chances are that Joe would thank this officious so-and-so to mind his own business and let him buy his own mower.

This book will explore the handling of these two types in another chapter, but with regard to qualifying, this must be exposed at the start, or you might wind up with several hours spent practicing for nothing. Besides, practice on this type you don't need anyway.

The question as to who the buyer is applies to the company sale more than anything else. The fellow you're talking to may be looking for a fleet of trucks or the supplies to outfit a 450-foot ocean tanker for his company. He may be the officially-designated buyer who needs *no other approval* to give you the order. So be careful when he says, "I'm not looking for myself." He might not be; he might be looking for the local paper mill as its purchasing agent.

Before leaving this aspect of qualifying, a simple method of being sure of who this fellow is is to make a quick call to his alleged company.

Ask for the purchasing agent. If they say he's out ask for his name by telling them you're new in town and haven't met him yet. If the name matches or if they tell you that they don't have a purchasing agent, but Mr. Jones, your prospect's name, does most of the buying, you're in business. If not, it *might* call for further checking before you go on.

An experienced salesman can tell as much about a person simply be looking as he can by talking or asking questions, usually. The trick here is not to be fooled by appearance; just *use it* to prepare for the approach you're going to take in asking your questions.

By the same token that a barefoot, long-haired hippie-type is not a likely prospect for a $40,000 life insurance policy, the fact that a man wears work clothes or is in need of a shave doesn't mean that he isn't able to buy that same policy.

The discerning salesman can usually spot a phoney by listening, not only to what he says, but the way he says it. After all, it won't be hard to spot a man who claims to be a graduate engineer if he speaks like a bowery bum. It just doesn't figure.

Again, don't be fooled by the manner of speech. It, too, can be misleading, and cause you to make a wrong snap judgment.

Also important in the overall qualifying procedure are the little things. If he comes to you, note the car he drives, count the children, and take a look at his wife. Is she tailored, hair set recently, nice diamond?

If you go to his place of business, look at his rolling stock, count his employees, and see whether he has a receptionist and/or secretary. How does his office look? Are there modern machines, or are they outdated? Do his employees look busy, or are they *trying* to look busy?

Here again, don't be fooled by the prospect's appearance. Remember the picture of Adlai Stevenson, candidate for president? It was much the same—the soles of both shoes worn through, an indication that he might not be completely solvent, much less a qualified candidate for the presidency, and a multimillionaire in his own right.

Of course you wouldn't list these questions. Sit the prospect down and feed them to him carefully. The answers come from slipping the questions into the conversation one at a time until you have all the answers, a picture of what your prospect is, and what he can or cannot do. Then you are ready to proceed or stop as the *answers* and your *experience* dictate.

A Typical Qualification

The man is about thirty-five, neat, and well dressed. He's driving a late model car, not brand new, and it too is clean and well cared for. The car is registered in another county (You know how to check this), and has a two-way aerial on its rear fender.

A typical conversation might sound like this:

"Where do you work, Mr. Jones? Are you one of those lucky people who never work Saturday?"

"No such luck. I'm with the highway department."

"Oh, a policeman?"

"No, nothing as exciting as that. I'm an engineer. My home is in Oakville (you recognize this as a town 250 miles away), and I'm staying down here until we get the new throughway finished. Be glad to get back to the family, too. I miss not being with the little fellow every night like I used to."

"I know what you mean, sir. How old is he?"

"Six."

"Cute age. You enjoy them when they're little, don't you? Best I remember Oakville is a small town. Guess he has a nice big yard to tear around in. That's always good for a youngster, especially a lively boy."

"We have a big yard, yes. Bought the house two years ago. My wife was scared he'd get in the highway, so she made me build a fence. He can't do much 'tearing around' though. He was born with a birth defect and has to wear a brace."

"Oh, I'm sorry, Mr. Jones. I didn't. . .the poor kid!"

"It's all right. You didn't know. He's better, anyway. Doctors say he's almost out of the woods. Say he'll play baseball yet. That's what I want the boat and motor for. Might help for him to get out on the water now and then. Maybe learn to ski and that sort of thing. Should be good for the muscles."

"Yes, sir! Best thing in the world for the little tyke. In fact, I have something here that would just suit. . . ."

Notice how the salesman had only to ask one major question, "Where do you work?" and one minor one, "How old is your son?" and he had all the answers he needed to determine that this man could be sold a fine boat and motor, and probably accessories and a trailer to go with them.

He had found out that the man was an engineer, a college man judging from his job and his speech. He had found out that he was married, had bought a home in a small town some miles distant, and that he loved his family; wanted to buy a boat for his crippled son.

The Other Side of the Coin

The man is about the same age, needs a shave and has, from the smell of his breath, been drinking. His clothes are soiled and cheap, and the car he's driving is an old model, beat-up and dirty. Its license shows it to be registered locally.

"Where do you work, Mr. Craven?"

"Highway Department."

"Oh, a policeman?"

"I ain't no blasted cop. I work for the maintenance department. Wouldn't have a job as a stinkin' cop for nobody. How much is that rig over there?" He points to a $5,000 outfit with twin inboard-outboards and all the trimmings.

"That's a nice rig. Where do you live, Mr. Craven? Here in town?"

"Live in the project. S'all I can afford since that no-good wife of mine took off with the kids a year ago. Court takes all I make to feed the brats. She ain't sick like she tells the judge, either. Fakin', that's all. Fakin' so he won't make her go to work. I could prove she's fakin' if they'd give me about ten minutes with her, you know? How much you say that rig is?"

"How long have you been with the highway department, Mr. Craven? A long time, I'll bet."

"Not too long. Four years, a little better. Thinkin' of changin'. I'm on a six-month suspension right now. Said I was drinkin' on the job just 'cause they don't like me. Said I wrecked the truck 'cause I was drunk. How was I to know it was a one-way street? Huh? I ask you, how was I to know they had changed the. . . ."

No need to go any further. By asking the questions directly, the salesman invariably got more information than he asked for; incriminating evidence that showed quite clearly that it was very doubtful that this man could buy *any* boat, much less the expensive one he was asking about.

He was a drinker and had been suspended from his job for drinking. His wife had left him and had been awarded custody of the children. He was living in the project because that was the "best he could afford." His drinking must have been quite serious. He had wrecked a truck, and with four years on the job he had still been suspended. His "thinking about changing" probably meant he soon would be, or had already been, fired. Also, he was looking at a boat that cost three times what even a good family man and worker in his job could afford.

The Somebody Else Shopper

The answers to these questions can be elicited from the housewife shopping for her husband or the man looking around for his boss or friend in much the same way. "Where does your husband (boss) work?", and "how many children do you folks have, Mrs. Perkins?" will get the answers just as easily as they're gotten from the prospect himself. In this case the *name* and *telephone number* of the *real prospect* is *most important of all.*

Get All the Facts—and the Sale

One of the most productive and successful salesmen I know is with a mutual fund company. One day his telephone rang and a man asked whether Jim could come to his place of business to discuss a fund program, that he was too busy to leave.

My friend agreed to see him later that day, and was given the address of a garage on the edge of town. He went over that afternoon, and found a shabby, run-down, corrugated building with junk cars strewn everywhere. He got out, sure he had the wrong address.

A young fellow came out of the shop and asked whether he could help him.

When Jim told him he was looking for Mr. Jones, the fellow wiped his hands on a rag, offered his hand and said, "I'm Jones. You must be the man from the mutual fund company."

Jim was disgusted. He had obviously driven all this way for nothing, and would probably be lucky to get a ten dollar monthly contract out of this fellow. He didn't look as if he was getting enough to eat, much less have money to invest. The kicker?

The man's wife and baby had been killed two years before in an unfortunate accident, and the fellow had just settled the claim *for $315,000.*

Jim took four months investigating and checking various funds and setting up an investment program for the garage owner, to the tune of almost a quarter of a million dollars, for which he will receive regular commissions as long as the fund is in existence, or until Jim dies.

The Paper-Mill Worker

There was the man, fifty-odd, who told me that he worked at the local paper mill and that he wanted to buy three new cars, one for himself, a convertible for his daughter and a station wagon for his, as he put it, "garden-club wife." Most mill jobs pay from $125 to $150 per week. As I speculated that he'd better have a wad of cash, I recalled seeing a name similar to his in the paper a day or two before. I excused myself, called a friend who worked at the mill and was told that the name *wasn't similar* that it was *the same,* and he had recently been named superintendent and vice president of the mill—a $40,000 a year job.

Low Income?

Then there was the guy who said he lived in the city project, a low-income, low-rent development (you can't make over $40 a week and live there). The kicker was that he was *the manager* of the 4000-unit project and could buy anything he wanted, including the insurance agency, had he been so inclined.

The fellow who said he "worked out of the county manager's office," failed to tell the salesman, a boy I was training, that he *was* the county manager.

Cracks like "His credit is probably so bad they wouldn't take his cash" and "He still owes for last year's girl scout cookies" are fun to pass the time, but they *will* let you fall into a bad habit; *qualifying from the seat of your pants.*

How to Lose the Big Sale—Without Trying

In my files is a clipping from the local paper concerning a salesman at an agency in Atlanta. It seems that a fellow came into the showroom, asked to see the cheapest four-door sedan the company had, and then asked two questions. How soon could he get thirty of them, all one color, with vinyl interiors, and how much would they cost?

The salesman, a young fellow who fancied himself a real pro, noticed the man's stained khaki work clothes, his stout work shoes and greasy work cap, and excused himself to "get the figures from the boss." Of course he disappeared, satisfied that the man was a nut that couldn't buy a bicycle, much less thirty automobiles.

The man waited a few minutes for the salesman to come back with the figures he had requested, and left, telling another salesman that he was in a hurry. Before he left he gave that salesman his name and telephone number, instructing him to tell the other man that he would be at the number two hours later, and for him to call with delivery dates and prices.

The salesman waited until the fellow was gone and came out of hiding. When he saw the name and telephone number he tossed it in the waste basket without looking at it, muttering about "the nuts who take up a man's time for nothing."

A few days later a competitor down the street took an order for the thirty cars, the salesman earned a commission of $1,500 and the manager bought him the $100 suit of his choice as a bonus.

The "nut" had just sold   large tract of industrial property and was establishing a taxi company.

The Six Costly Mistakes

If you re-read the cases above, dealing with the misses and near misses caused by this type qualifying, you'll see that they cover *basic errors* that every salesman will make unless *he has a plan*.

In the case of the young boy, I made the most common error of all: qualifying by appearance. The boy was young, therefore he couldn't buy. No effort to find out whether he had been sent there by his father, someone who could buy; just a fast brush-off and back to the paper; he's too young. Loss of sale. The man who bought the thirty cars was the same. Something else: who is your prospect shopping *for*? His boss, who *can* buy, might have sent him out gathering prices while he attended to more important business.

Jim almost committed the same error when he sold the huge mutual fund folio; that of judging by appearance. Here a single, simple factor, a law suit settlement, converted a not-possible to a definite.

The man from the paper mill didn't want to walk in and yell, "Hey, I'm the new vice president of the paper mill and I want to buy three new cars." He wanted a salesman with a *planned approach* to ask him *where he worked* and *what his job* was so he could get it across that he *could,* and *was going to,* buy three cars.

The county manager and the fellow managing the city project were in much the same position. The salesman found out by accident and pure luck that he had a good chance for a sale if he played his cards right.

Remember the six questions that eliminate luck. The secret lies in the fact that *the qualification technique is not complete until all the questions have been covered.* Of course the first answer might be an indication that the prospect can or cannot buy, but not definitely, and that's what we're after.

We're setting up a *foolproof plan* that will show us whether to stick with this prospect or to drop him and look for another.

Qualifying the Commercial Buyer

What about the buyer for a company, for the proprietor himself? You don't care what the buyer's salary is, or whether he has good credit. You're interested in his *company* and *their* needs.

Or in the case of the proprietor buying for his company you need to know about both the company, and him personally.

The information you need is basically the same, but you get it in a different way.

Reference Books That Help in Qualifying

There are several books which will lay the preliminary ground work and are indispensible to the salesman. The initial interview will get the rest of what he needs to qualify the firm and/or the proprietor.

All of the *telephone books* in his sales territory, as well as a *city directory* should be available to him. A current copy of *Dun and Bradstreet's Rating Book* and a *credit rating* from the *local bureau* should be at his fingertips.

Most companies have these books in their offices, and those that don't certainly *should* have them. If the company doesn't have a local credit rating book, or if the credit bureau doesn't provide one (many don't), the salesman should be authorized to run credit checks on any firm or proprietor who he feels might be a potential prospect, without having to get permission from anyone. Subscriptions to trade journals, as well as a copy of *Who's Who in American Business* are also very valuable to the sales force selling to companies.

Another simple trick helpful to the salesman doing business with companies, large or small, is to go by the plant and see for himself. There he can see what the operation looks like, and possibly determine whether or not they are able to purchase the equipment, machinery or inventory they're considering.

Condensing these comments on qualifying into a sentence or two is difficult. It is too important, and too involved to sum it up in a few words.

However, there is a list of reminders that apply in *every qualifying situation,* regardless of the product or the type of prospect.

But before we get into the do's and don't we've covered on the qualifying technique, this is also important:

In the qualifying portion of the sales approach, your attitude is as important as it is *at any time* during the confrontations with the prospect.

Don't make the mistake of deciding to return to the paper because the prospect is young, or tell him that he's wasting his time because he's just gotten out of jail.

When that prospect (we covered this more fully in another chapter) comes in, or when you arrive at his office to keep an appointment, be sure you approach him as a *potential buyer* as a person who might be hard to sell, but for you a person who can be *sold,* difficult or not.

To sum it up we have the following basic rules to remember:

Don't try to qualify from the seat of your pants.

Don't let one discouraging feature or one discouraging answer to one of the six basic questions stop you.

Don't jump to conclusions or pre-judge your prospect or his company.

Do get all the facts before you decide—either way.

Do be sure you have the answers to all six questions before you decide.

Do, in the case of a company, get the facts before you go for the sales interview. You can learn a lot just driving by the plant.

Do, again in the case of a company, get the city directory, the necessary telephone books, *Dun and Bradstreet* and credit ratings so you can go for the interview armed with the facts you need to be able to present a good close to the purchasing agent or the proprietor.

He will be flattered and will see that he's dealing with a *professional* who knows his business when you are able to quote facts about his company and its standing.

13

Thirty One-Line Big League Reminders That Will Help to Make You a Better Closer

These one-liners are the result of an article I wrote for *The American Salesman,* entitled "Use the Card and Sell." It described my most difficult sales problem and the solution which I devised to control that problem. The problem was staying "up," under all conditions, and no matter how I felt. This was not a problem unique to me, as I knew and know many salesmen who suffer from it. None, I'm sure, were worse than I was, though.

Then, one day I realized that I had licked the worst of it simply by realizing what my problem was; that all I needed was the counter-measure that would lick or at least control it.

Then I hit on an idea so simple as to be almost silly, but it worked. A wallet card—actually, the first one I made was printed on the back of my business card—with the legend, "I am the *best salesman in this firm.* I am going to *prove* that *on this prospect.* I am *going* to *sell him.* I am *going to SMILE.*"

From that day on the card was in my hand as I approached a prospect. It wasn't long before I found that I wasn't even looking at it; that I was unconciously repeating what I call my "smile reminder." I also found my sales increasing accordingly.

It soon developed that I was helping the other men set their problems and their reminder down on a card, and showing them how to use it.

Carl's problem was pre-judging his prospect—qualifying before he had the facts. Louie talked too much, while Ed was like me; he let the blues get him down. Every one of them learned to control (these are usually deep-seated personality traits that can rarely be changed, but can be controlled) his problem by using the card.

Many men found that they couldn't pinpoint their worst fault, and new men didn't know what it might be; so I prepared a set of 30 cards, one for each day of the month. The object was to carry one each day, and thus cause the real culprit to show itself. Some of us found there were several things on which we needed constant reminders, while some just one. Either way, we found that the card worked, and that after a while the reminder became second nature and we didn't need to read the words.

Make up a set of these cards, or pick out the ones you need—your sales manager and the men you work with can often see faults you can't—and *use them.* You'll find yourself in *more closing situations,* and *closing more sales.*

1. Pull the key bricks from the brick overcoat of sales resistance and the coat will collapse.
2. If at first you don't succeed, tag.
3. Tagging the right man can mean the difference between a close and a miss.
4. For an easier close, tell a story, but not a lie.
5. Nod your head: A positive approach is the best approach.
6. You control the conversation and you'll get the close.
7. Offer your prospect a choice: never a yes-or-no.
8. Do it all now; an incomplete close is not a close at all.
9. Don't argue. You might win and blow the close.
10. If you never want to see your prospect again, sell him something he doesn't need.
11. Identify with the prospect and watch the bricks fall.
12. Women are easy to close if you remember they are women.
13. Never leave the closing room without three more prospects' names.
14. Flattery at the close will (usually) get you everywhere.
15. Invest a small portion of your earnings in future sales; it pays.
16. When you prepare the file on Mr. Jones make one on his brother-in-law, as well.

17. You can't qualify that prospect from the seat of your pants.

18. Time spent with an unqualified prospect is time wasted. Time is all you have to help you at the close.

19. Seeing is believing: demonstrate.

20. Closing a family, sell each member according to his needs or wants.

21. The professional buyer wants facts, not claims or opinions.

22. Prospecting is a seven days per week must for the successful salesman.

23. The number of closing situations you find yourself in will be inversely proportional to the number of hours spent on the seat of your pants.

24. When the closing effort bogs down, the double-team might pull it out of the bog.

25. The first close is not nearly as valuable as the ones in the future. Keep a file.

26. Smile, and get more closes.

27. Keep the conversation on the target: the close.

28. Press the go-button before the prospect is ready and it will be the blow-button.

29. When you stop closing you stop eating.

30. If you knock off when the sales room closes you're in the wrong profession; selling is a full-time job.

31. This is your bonus reminder: overhaul your closing techniques constantly and you'll be a better closer, and will spend more commissions.

Index

A

Abusiveness in customer, how to handle, 63-65

Accidental tag, 62-65

Adjustment of salesman to prospect, psychology of, 35-48
  gladiators, analogy of, 35-36
  "slap his face" advice, 30-42
  specializing, 46-48
  "switch," 45-46
  "two-hat" approach, 42-44

Advance planning helpful in getting close, 89-90

Advertising not necessarily salesman, 79-80

Alienation of customer danger in knocking competition, 129

American Salesman, 191

Appearance of prospect, using criterion of in qualifying, 181

Approaches to close, four basic, 98-107
  demonstration, 101-104
  interest of prospect, emphasizing, 99-100
  outside influence, 104-106
  telling you, prospect's, what you are selling, 100-102

Arguing with customer fatal to sale, 123-125

Authority, assuming, often fatal error in closing sales, 132-133

Authority added to persuasion to work against prospect blackout, 117-119

"Authority" tag, 50-54

Avoiding errors in closing, 123-137
  "boss," playing, 132-133
  competition, knocking, 128-132
  "don't" of avoiding other "don'ts," 136-137
  opinions, offering, 125-128
  oversell, 134-136
  payments, 136
  "you're wrong, Mr. Jones," attitudes, 123-125

B

Back-in methods of guarding against prospect backout, 114-122
  "do-nothing" approach, 116-117
  double-team, standard, 119-120
  "feet to the fire" approach, 121-122
  guilty conscience of prospect, capitalizing on, 115-116
  "last day" approach, 120-121
  "no messages" approach, 117
  persuasion plus authority, 117-119
  preparing for, 122

"Backlash" effect of knocking competition often fatal for sale, 129

Backout of prospect, six ways to prevent, 109-122
  (see also "Prospect backout. . .")

Belligerence in customer, how to handle, 63-65

"Boss," playing, often fatal error in closing sale, 132-133